Continuing the Journey

Continuing the Journey is a five-book series on advanced approaches to teaching English language arts. Written for veteran teachers by Leila Christenbury and Ken Lindblom, the books include "From the Teachers' Lounge," an innovative feature that honors the expertise of both colleagues from the field and highly regarded scholars. Topics addressed in the series include literature and informational texts; language and writing; listening, speaking, and presenting; digital literacies; and living the professional life of a veteran teacher.

IN THIS SERIES

Continuing the Journey 2: Becoming a Better Teacher of Authentic Writing (2018)
Continuing the Journey: Becoming a Better Teacher of Literature and Informational Texts (2017)

Continuing the Journey 2

*Becoming a Better Teacher of
Authentic Writing*

Ken Lindblom

Stony Brook University, State University of New York

Leila Christenbury

Virginia Commonwealth University, Richmond

**National Council of
Teachers of English**

1111 W. Kenyon Road, Urbana, Illinois 61801-1096
www.ncte.org

Staff Editor: Bonny Graham

Interior Design: Ashlee Goodwin

Cover Design: Pat Mayer

NCTE Stock Number: 08574; eStock Number: 08598

ISBN 978-0-8141-0857-4; eISBN 978-0-8141-0859-8

©2018 by the National Council of Teachers of English.

Every effort has been made to provide current URLs and email addresses, but because of the rapidly changing nature of the web, some sites and addresses may no longer be accessible.

Library of Congress Cataloging-in-Publication Data

A catalog record of this book has been requested.

To my beautiful sister, Denise, who always keeps me humble.
To my unique brother, Tim, who always keeps me guessing.
—*Ken*

To Tucker. Always.
—*Leila*

CONTENTS

Contents

Foreword

There is nothing like life in the classroom.

What a gift it is to spend our days in the classroom with students. Anyone who has worked alongside students knows what an exciting journey teaching is. But it is also a journey that includes difficult times as well. Staying grounded and energized is sometimes a challenge for veteran teachers.

As Ken and Leila say in the introduction to this new book, "There is no more challenging a job than ours. There is also no job more important." For those of us who are veteran teachers, we know how true this is. The journey of a teacher is a lifelong journey. We learn quickly that this job is about always learning, always growing, always reflecting. As a classroom teacher for more than thirty years, my journey continues each day.

I know this to be true: the key to sustaining joy is in the authenticity we bring to the classroom. In these challenging times, we have to work to be more intentional about making sure our work with students is authentic.

Continuing the Journey 2: Becoming a Better Teacher of Authentic Writing is all about authenticity. Leila and Ken take us on another journey in which we think about ways to stay current and authentic when it comes to writing instruction.

Let's face it, writing instruction is always changing. There are new tools, new ways to share, new and better ways to connect to other writers. But the things we know about teaching writing help us to remain grounded with all of these changes.

Leila and Ken help us to see the power in staying current as well as the importance in staying grounded in our beliefs. They know that those two things create writing classrooms where teachers—who are writers themselves—continue to be energized and passionate, and students find joy and purpose in writing in direct reflection of their teachers.

This lens of authenticity threads through this entire book. Not only is authentic writing important, but Leila and Ken know the power of authentic relationships with students. They know that learning from and with other teachers is essential to each teaching journey. In this new book, we come to know several teachers in the Teachers' Lounge—a feature that runs through the book, highlighting the voices of classroom teachers and their own experiences.

NCTE is lucky to have Ken and Leila as leaders, and I feel lucky to have them as mentors on this teaching journey. May the thinking in this book, and present in each teacher voice contained in the pages, enrich you in the same ways it does me.

Franki Sibberson, President
National Council of Teachers of English

Acknowledgments

Writing a book is always a group effort. This book, the second in the Continuing the Journey series, is probably even more so, as may be obvious from the number of names listed on the cover.

We are grateful for NCTE's support of this work, and particularly to Executive Director Emily Kirkpatrick, for her continuous encouragement and enthusiasm for the project. She is a savvy and powerful leader, and we NCTE members are fortunate to have her at the helm.

In addition to Emily Kirkpatrick, Kurt Austin and Bonny Graham provide excellent editing and production management, ensuring countless stars align for this work to be published professionally and in a timely manner. Many thanks to them. We also appreciate the NCTE peer reviewers' feedback and suggestions, all of which made this a stronger book.

Of course, we are delighted to thank all those colleagues who made a stop in our ideal Teachers' Lounge: Jennifer Ansbach, Jim Burke, Deborah Dean, Patricia A. Dunn, Ellen Foley, Lorena Germán, Nancy Mack, Alison McKeough, Kimberly N. Parker, Evelyn T. Pineiro, Dawn Reed, Christopher Scanlon, Andy Schoenborn, Nicole Sieben, Julia Torres, and Y'Shanda Young-Rivera. And we wish to thank other teaching colleagues, Emily Puccio and a few whose classrooms we have described and who wish to remain anonymous, whose views and experiences have enriched this work. Finally, we are delighted that NCTE President Franki Sibberson accepted our invitation to write a foreword to this volume. A truly gifted teacher-leader, Franki lends considerable gravitas to our effort.

There are also some personal thanks to offer. Ken sends his love and thanks to Patty Dunn, who is both his journey and destination, filling both with laughter, music, and love. Ken also thanks for her support, her patient ear, and her energetic voice his mother, Anne

Russell. And he thanks his siblings, Denise Sullivan and Tim Lindblom, to whom he dedicates this book. No one is there for you quite like a sibling; in Denise, Tim, and Ken's case, all too many childhood battles in too-close quarters have healed over, providing rich foundation for a lifetime of friendship and support. (I know: *Gag!*)

Leila thanks Tucker for his sense of humor and unfailing support, and she promises, now that this project is over, to spend more time with four-footed friends Enzo and Mimi, who have felt neglected but are too dignified to mention it.

Finally, we thank all our English teaching colleagues, for whom we write and with whom we commune, converse, and collaborate. Teaching English well takes brains, endurance, patience, creativity, and optimism. Thank goodness there are so many we know who are not only well up to the challenge but whose examples continue to inspire us.

CHAPTER 1

The Power of Teaching Authentic Writing

Holden Caulfield, the main character in J. D. Salinger's classic novel *The Catcher in the Rye*, is obsessed, as many young people are, with being honest, with being authentic. He hates the fake, the façade, what he calls the *phony*. For Holden, the adults who surround him are the phonies, and he is determined not to be one of them. He prides himself on having what he calls a *bullshit detector*, and for decades the readers of *Catcher in the Rye*—especially adolescents—have loved Holden for that.

With the armor of age, the perspective of the years, we can chuckle a bit at Holden, at his youthful intransigence, at his assurance that he is morally right, at his occasional extremism. But in our classrooms, Holden lives and walks among us, and even today he has much to teach us.

For us, Ken and Leila, no matter how many years have passed since we have taught full-time in a secondary classroom, a great number of the students we know share Holden's obsession. In our daily teaching, our students live with us, and we are adults who are close to them every day. As they work with us, they observe us, judge us, and, along the way, often want to know what truly motivates us. They don't want us to give them the party line, the official version, the sanitized story; they want the real deal. To be real, to be honest, to be *authentic,* is a mandatory quality for an effective teacher, and when we teach the Holdens in our schools, we must be mindful of these basic requirements. Our students demand it. And, truth be told, we should, every day, demand it of ourselves.

I

If we are inauthentic, we find ourselves justifying ill-conceived school rules, traditional courses of study, or other questionable aspects of school and adult life with specious and even laughably half-hearted comments: *You'll thank me after graduation; You'll need this in later life; It's how we've always done this; Don't ask questions; It's just how it is;* or, the worst (we think): *Because I said so.* Aspects of some of these comments may be true, but the fact is they are also evasions and false contentions even at that.

To hew to the essential and the right, to teach with the sincere knowledge that what we are doing with our students and in our classrooms is truly useful and central and defensible, is to teach authentically. As veteran teachers, we are charged with putting that authenticity center stage; if at one time in our careers we were fearful or hesitant and we always enforced the rules, no matter what we thought of them, now is the time to shed those insecurities.

In the English classroom in particular there is a unique opportunity to enact authenticity in writing. This skill and area of study is essential to education and, indeed, to success in later life, but only if what we teach realistically reflects the world beyond school. Spending time with our students crafting accurate and effective arguments, using precise and targeted vocabulary, and shifting our discourse to meet specific audiences and purposes is central to our work with our students and central to what the world beyond school expects of them.

And so we want to make clear at the outset that this book revolves around authenticity and how it guides and shapes the real-world teaching of writing and language. We also know you will find yourself in these pages, and we are excited to be with you on this continuing journey.

Our deep belief is that veteran teachers should be beacons of authenticity, and in this book we explore why and how. As one of our colleague reviewers, Darren Crovitz, noted:

> Most of the writing students do in conventional classrooms is inauthentic; redesigning curricula and pedagogy around the principle of authenticity means questioning a variety of common assumptions and reshaping the writing classroom in fundamental ways. In particular, authenticity presumes a different kind of teaching and student persona that challenges us to teach writing through

community building, shared struggle over time, honest discussions of craft and quality, and a constant focus on real-world audiences and publication.

We could not have said it any better.

WHAT DOES IT MEAN TO TEACH WRITING AS A VETERAN ENGLISH TEACHER?

If indeed you would see yourself as an avatar of authenticity, consider whether the following paragraph describes you and your teaching.

No longer afraid of grade challenges or overbearing administrators, you are comfortable in your classroom. The students respect your authority, and they generally do what you tell them. You have a few years of lesson plans to fall back on, and you don't have trouble taking some risks here and there. You're a veteran. You've arrived. Time to relax into your teaching style and ride the back–and-forths of the education pendulum each year till summer break and then into a well-earned early retirement.

Chances are you're already calling *baloney* on the preceding paragraph, confirming that your own version of Holden's bullshit detector still works. No, we do not believe that you are one to rest on your laurels and coast on your confidence. Still, it's easy for veteran teachers to let a few years' experience settle them into complacency, and if you add to that the current political turmoil affecting almost all aspects of public and national education, one can understand the desire for a head-in-the-sand approach to almost all educational issues.

So is there a downside to being an assured veteran? It may well be that feeling too comfortable is not a positive but a danger, as teacher and blogger Tom Rademacher says: "There's no better sign that things are going poorly in a room than a teacher who always thinks everything is going just fine" ("My Name" n.p.).

We trust this is not you. Good veteran teachers know that each year brings new students for whom we may be their best hope for a successful future. Young people's literacy development is too important for us to simply forge ahead regardless of the complexities of this year's cohort of students. So yes, once we as teachers have reached a certain level of comfort and security in the classroom, it's actually our responsibility to challenge ourselves, to learn and undertake best practices in teaching even if—especially if—those best practices are misunderstood by the general public and discouraged by administrators, parents, education reformers, other teachers, and even our students. In short, we no longer have our inexperience and insecurity to fall back on as an excuse—or, truly, as a defensible reason—for playing it safe. Teaching English well as a veteran teacher is inherently risky work.

In the first volume of the Continuing the Journey series, we took on advanced approaches to teaching literature and informational texts (Christenbury and Lindblom, *Continuing*). We explored ways of bringing to students highly complex texts that raise the bar on their effort. We examined how real-world texts can engage reluctant students in literature. We looked at ways that informational text can enhance literature and stand on its own. We suggested methods for treating social media as a medium and content for English classes. And we explored the risks involved in teaching contemporary texts and the rough and unforgiving world of social and political discourse. In this book, the second leg of our continuing journey, we focus on writing, a subject that when taught well can be every bit as controversial as an adult-themed novel. We won't be shy about what research has taught us about writing, concepts deeply rooted in personal identity and real-world experience, and why we must teach them accurately, effectively, and fearlessly.

As in the previous volume, we'll make frequent stops in our ideal Teachers' Lounge, where we'll encounter highly experienced colleagues and well-known authors in English teaching. Their advice will help illustrate and in some cases challenge what we, Ken and Leila, have to say. We trust you'll find this journey supportive, encouraging, and (re)invigorating, and that it will inspire you to more authentic teaching of writing.

WHAT DOES IT MEAN TO TEACH WRITING AUTHENTICALLY?

WHEN I FIRST STARTED *teaching high school English, I was assigned a senior class called College Writing Skills. I had not been taught anything about how to teach writing, a common situation way back when I earned teacher certification. I found a text in the*

bookroom—remember searching through bookrooms?!—that I thought might do the trick. The book included several essays in which the iden-tified topic sentence of each paragraph was removed, and that sentence, along with three other less suitable choices, was listed in a multiple-choice quiz at the end of each essay. There were ten essays, which meant I could assign two essays per class, which meant a whole week of lesson plans was all set and done. It was an amazing week, and all the students were thrilled. By the end, they all knew how to write the best topic sentences ever!

Nope. Not even close.

This class was so boring that the students got understandably hostile the second day I handed those books out. Already nervous with se-niors, I capitulated quickly—I was so young looking that the high school principal had to bring me on stage during a faculty meeting to keep my new colleagues from yelling at me in the hallway! I don't recall what I did next, but I know that poor first group of students never got a decent day of writing instruction from me.

What Ken just described is distinctly NOT authentic writing instruction. First, he de-fined writing using an artificial construct that doesn't really exist outside a language labora-tory: "topic sentence." Second, the students were required to use writing that came from an outdated, not very interesting workbook. Third, the students were not asked to do anything meaningful with the writing; in fact, they weren't even writing—in a class about learning to write! Although Ken later learned a lot more about teaching writing well, you as a veteran English teacher won't be shocked to learn that all of his formal teaching observations that first year (which he got to arrange and select, not to mention plan ahead for) were focused on literature lessons.

Authentic writing is real writing, written for a real audience, for a real purpose, in a real forum. For example:

- A letter to an editor for a specific newspaper, written by a student about an issue she or he cares about

- A presentation to the board of education written and presented by a group of students to argue for funds for an art club, to petition the principal to sponsor an LGBT night, or to request funds from a local sporting goods store to start a hunting club

- A class blog about school issues written and read by students, teachers, and administrators

But *teaching* authentic writing means more than coming up with interesting assignments. It means creating a writing community. Leila explains:

 I THINK IT CAN *be easy to talk about authenticity and being honest with students but, for me, at least, it has been a learned skill and not one that has come readily. What could I tell my students about writing that was genuine? Not much, because I felt for many years that I needed to keep my private struggles to myself. Early in my career, I did not want my students to know that my own writing history was a checkered one. I wanted so to succeed, but as a student I struggled throughout almost all my school years—my poetry was lame, my short fiction was plotless, and as I worked on essays and research papers, I found that using elevated diction and vocabulary could mask my lack of structure and argument. I almost lost all confidence my last semester of college when my honors thesis crashed on the rocks and I feared I would*

never complete it. Luckily, I did, but the final writing was forced, stilted, and did not reflect at all what I thought I had wanted to say.

But I kept at it, and when in graduate school I had to write every week and meet multiple deadlines, something broke open. I found I could write, and write well and quickly. And so when I read in the professional literature about the power of writing with your students, I was, for once, all in. The formats changed with the times, but the classroom writing did not: on the board (using chalk), on the overhead (using acetate and a marker), on the document camera (using paper and pen), on the computer (projected on a whiteboard), I wrote my drafts in class, in real time, where students could watch as I composed. I then read what I had written aloud and briefly discussed my writing choices and goofs and bloopers.

This was one of the best things I ever did in my teaching of writing. Writing a first draft with students was beyond powerful; students noticed, and while they didn't praise my work—it was truly first draft stuff, and there was no reason to pretend otherwise—the feeling of a shared enterprise was demonstrated convincingly. Without preaching, without lecturing, without posturing, it was clear that I, the teacher, was a writer with my students. The sense of a community as I wrote with them established the writing class atmosphere and gave my teaching of writing the authenticity I knew was necessary.

Our colleague and veteran English teacher Deborah Dean agrees: it's really about getting students to see themselves as writers. Wouldn't it be great to hear from Dean in her own words? We're in luck. The author of the well-received *Strategic Writing: The Writing Process and Beyond in the Secondary English Classroom* (2nd ed.), *Genre Theory: Teaching, Writing, and Being*, and other popular titles has time right now to chat with us in our ideal Teachers' Lounge.

FROM THE TEACHERS' LOUNGE

Make Students the Focus of Authenticity

Deborah Dean
Brigham Young University, Provo, Utah

As an early career teacher, I thought the only interpretation of teaching writing authentically was to have students send writing to audiences outside the classroom. I had my students write letters of compliment or complaint that they sent to businesses. They wrote letters to the editor of the local newspaper and saw themselves in print. As successful as those experiences were, the practice was hard to do: it was difficult to find authentic audiences, and I wasn't sure students saw themselves as writers from these limited experiences.

Last summer I found a list that my second-grade granddaughter left behind after her family took a very early morning flight. The list was titled "List to go to Arazona [sic]" and had these items in a column: "put PJs in suitcase, get dressed, eat toast, brush hair in car to airport, get on plane, read, draw, play, read, draw, play, read, draw, play."

To me, this example exemplifies the goal I eventually developed for my students. Authentic writing instruction isn't only about finding audiences beyond me or their classmates; it's about developing writers who see themselves as writers who use writing for real purposes in their lives. I needed to make students *the focus of authenticity.*

To teach writing toward that goal means, first, that students don't see writing in my class as simply completing assignments. It means that the genres we write in class exist in the world outside of school. It means giving students room to make some choices in their writing: in the topics, genres, processes, and language options they use. It means they should have personal goals they are working to improve, not just learning out-comes determined by me, the district, or the state. In all, authentic writing in school means that students get to make some choices and use writing to do things—not only to show what they know or know how to do.

Teaching writing authentically also means that students see me us-ing writing in meaningful and purposeful ways, with all the messiness and struggle that entails. I share my writing successes and failures. Students see me writing in my writer's notebook, revising and publishing, trying the same tasks I ask them to consider. Sometimes I bring a piece I am having trouble with and ask what they think I should do. I write in front of them, taking risks, and they see me doing it.

When I teach writing authentically, I know that sometimes students' writing will not be as successful as it could have been had I made more of the choices for them. Becoming a writer is mostly a messy process, full of stops and starts, risks that succeed and ones that don't. To me, though, teaching writing authentically is more about my students' development as writers than the success of a particular piece of writing or the score on a standardized writing test. If my students see writing as pur-poseful in their lives and see themselves as writers, like my granddaughter, then I feel that I've succeeded in teaching writing authentically.

ENHANCING AUTHENTIC INSTRUCTION IN WRITING AND LANGUAGE

Here are some ways we have enhanced our own writing instruction to be more authentic, to help students engage more in their own development as writers, which includes, of course, also expanding their exposure to language:

Writing

▸ Use authentic processes and authentic topics

- ▸ Write yourself

- ▸ Write in front of your students

- ▸ Use peer groups for revision

- ▸ Bring internet and social media writing into class

Language

- ▸ Bring internet and social media terms into class

- ▸ Acknowledge and work with the changes in language formality and acceptability

- ▸ Explore new words

Teaching language authentically is similar to teaching writing authentically. Instead of focusing solely on standardized English, an authentic language classroom focuses on language as it is actually used in varieties of contexts. Authentic language includes standardized English and the many other forms of English Language (see Chapter 8 for an explanation of our preference for this term) that function in the real world. Authentic language *contrasts* versions of English rather than *corrects* them (Wheeler). Students in classes that treat language authentically learn to use language to suit their own purposes in a range of real-world contexts.

Teachers who focus on authenticity do not try to break each student down and then remake him or her in a single image. They add to each student's language background so that students can function effectively in any social context in which they choose to be successful.

We're inspired by veteran teachers who find new ways to incorporate authentic writing into their classes. Let's take another trip to our Teachers' Lounge, where Nicole Sieben is waiting to tell us about how she uses authentic writing instruction to engage students in thinking and writing that encourages hope and empowers their future. In her recently published *Writing Hope Strategies for Writing Success in Secondary Schools: A Strengths-Based Approach to Teaching Writing*, Nicole outlines what she calls a Writing Hope Framework that underpins the concepts she describes here.

——— FROM THE TEACHERS' LOUNGE ———

Encouraging Hope with Writing Instruction

Nicole Sieben

SUNY College at Old Westbury, Old Westbury, New York

When we give students the space to write from a place of authenticity, we give them opportunities to build hope into their personal and professional narratives. Along with this increase in hope levels, writing competencies increase as well.

Allowing space in our classrooms for our students' own linguistic conventions and expressions sends a message of care to our students about how we value them as people with empowered voices in our classrooms and communities. If we force on students linguistic conventions that are teacher imposed, we do not give them the chance to express their individual goals and writing styles, inadvertently stunting students' hope-growth potential. Conversely, student-selected goals and discourses can magnify their hope-growth exponentially and can also tell us a great deal about how our students identify as writers and learners in the world.

Among those strengths-based discourses in education today is an empowering discourse of hope that can be woven into classroom conversations about authentic writing and being in the world. "Writing hope" is a vehicle for linguistic freedom, identity formation and exploration, and personal empowerment. It helps students (and all of us, really) to choose the pathways to self-defined success and propels writers forward in meaningful ways. With all of its intrinsic value, it's no wonder that writing-hope levels predict students' writing competency levels as well. When we place value on the things that really matter to our students— their goals, their voices, their cultures, their opinions, their audiences—we incite the use of those values in our classroom spaces, and we make room for student success to manifest in a variety of ways.

Encouraging our students to find, build, and maintain hope while writing shows them we are invested in their personal goals for the future and will support them in getting there. When we engage students in a practice of "nexting," in which we ask them to anticipate next steps, next challenges to overcome, next pathways, next successes, and next goals, we encourage a "future-casting" process that advances students in their writing in ways that are authentically powerful for each writer.

In my classroom, writing hope is omnipresent in our discourse community because it invites variety in writing process approaches, goal creation, and self-expression. Writing hope does not privilege one linguistic writing style over another; instead, it allows for a multitude of voices to be empowered within an equitably oriented system aimed at future goal pursuit for all students. Collectively, my students and I commit to recognizing hope in our work together, and we capitalize on hope moments for and with one another by celebrating the unique voices that contribute great value to our community of writers.

For example, in one of my composition courses, Women's Voices, I include an artifactual expository assignment in which students are invited to weave together two distinct linguistic styles authentic to their writing lives in order to describe an artifact of their identities/cultures/ histories that carries strong meaning for them. In an assignment that includes intentional code-meshing (using more than one style of discourse in the same communication), students' writing illuminates the beauty of embracing multiple facets of one voice and/or many voices.

As a partner in writing hope alongside my students, I share a consistent commitment to future-casting with the writers I have the humbling honor of working with throughout our time together.

CONCLUSION: TEACHING FOR AN UNCERTAIN WORLD

Drafting this introductory chapter sometime in spring 2018, we can't help but acknowledge and note that the strong voices of young people, in particular high school students, are newly important and significant to our culture. Some sixty years ago, young people (as well as adults) gathered in large groups and, in boisterous and loud voices, demanded justice, social change, and the end of an unpopular war. Today, sparked by the continuous and seemingly unstoppable incidents of gun violence enacted in schools, young people—and their language, their tweets, their presentations in front of banks of microphones, their testimony to state legislative bodies—are garnering attention to a significant issue in American life. These young people are the products of our English classes and our schools, and whether we have helped them find their voices or they are finding them despite us, the evidence of the Parkland, Florida, youth is powerful and underscores the importance—and the moral inevitability—of teaching authentic language and writing in our classes and in our schools. We can do no less than continue to engage students in responsible and authentic practices in our classrooms and in our daily instruction.

As veteran teachers, we have the standing to push for topics and discussions that our less senior colleagues may shun or even fear. For us, however, this kind of authenticity is ours to claim and our responsibility to claim for our important partners, the students. With the rapid advance of technology and the new political realities reshaping global and national relations, we are less sure than our teachers were in the past about what the future will bring our students. But we know we must prepare our students for whatever the future brings, and that means teaching in a way that engages with the world as it evolves.

In this book, we hope to provide background knowledge and pedagogical tools that will assist you as a veteran teacher in teaching writing in an authentic manner. We aim to provide greater explanations of complex theory; rubrics, handouts, assignment ideas, and other materials; and examples of authentic teaching from real-world classes. Finally, as you will have already noted, we will present wise words from colleagues across the country in our ideal Teachers' Lounge, for as a profession we are at our strongest when we actively listen to each other, learning from the experience of multitudes.

If we've done our jobs well, you'll find that this book and its contributors inspire, enhance, and perhaps challenge your teaching. You, like us, are a veteran teacher. You are well past those first-year jitters and are ready to accept the full force of the responsibility to educate your students for an uncertain and ever-changing world. There is no more challenging a job than ours. There is also no job more important.

What Does It Mean to Be a Better Teacher of Writing? Moving into the Real World

MAKING OUR CLASSROOMS RELEVANT

One of the great indictments of what happens in American schools and classrooms is that very little of what we do with students relates to anything remotely attached to what most people refer to as the "real" world. Critics charge that the skills school curricula require are often wholly institution based, useful only for school itself, and the kinds of regulations and rules students are asked to comply with are pertinent only to a school environment. Although the currently incessant drumbeat for twenty-first-century skills may indeed grate on us as classroom veterans, we may also agree that that movement is, to give it credit, an effort to ensure that what happens in school does not stay in school—that it moves into the outside and, at times, unpredictable and ever-changing real world.

So we argue that English is not just for English class: writing is relevant, especially as a social activity. To be authentic in our teaching, we need to release writing out into the world and to be open—in our classrooms—to how writing functions in the outside world.

In doing so, we become better teachers of writing, and we turn to what is real, relevant—that is, what is *authentic* in both writing and in the language we wield in writing.

What does it mean to be a better teacher of writing? Part of our stated concern is authenticity, ensuring that our students write real things, for real people, and that they use realistic language tailored to actual situations. Thus the skills we ask students to pursue must be contextual, must relate to a world that no longer sends paper letters but uses electronic emails and shorter platforms—e.g., texts, Twitter, Instagram. How can we spend a majority of our time on restrictive clauses and their punctuation (favorite test items our students may encounter) when national policy and international events are now often conveyed through short, condensed, and effective bursts of language phrases on social media? If our sole goal is higher test scores on multiple-choice questions that do not admit of a twenty-first century, then it is time to put this book down and do something else. If, however, there is some confidence that those test items are only a small part of our obligation to our students, then we need to move into the world and out of where many English texts would place us—and the latter would be somewhere around 1955.

In writing, moving into the world means being realistic about the processes of writing and the topic of writing, not setting students up for some fairy tale picture of how they should be producing prose and not asking them to write as authorities on areas in which they—and virtually everyone else—have no interest and no stake. It means that students must be given opportunities to write for multiple audiences, using multiple forms of English Language—not just one version designed by elites (standardized English)—to effect different kinds of change and express different kinds of ideas.

In their powerful *Writing Instruction in the Culturally Relevant Classroom*, Maisha T. Winn and Latrise P. Johnson recognize how authentic writing instruction in middle and high school can link culturally relevant teaching to students' agency as writers: "Culturally relevant writing makes students more capable writers in that they have the opportunity to recognize and write for authentic audiences and purposes that matter to them." With such an approach to writing instruction, they continue, "comes an expanded notion of literacy in which the voices, perspectives, and lived experiences of students are considered" (22).

The fact is that writing is being used today possibly more than ever, thanks largely to social media; even young people write more outside school than did previous generations (Lenhart, Arafeh, Smith, and Macgill). That language is a powerful and dominant force, and wielding it effectively is changing entire nations. We can be assured, of course, that emojis have not replaced our written communication; visual images are not the sole lingua franca. The popularity of internet memes demonstrates that the visuals have enhanced, not replaced, text. Written language is all around us, every day, on almost every platform—and we are in a golden age of sorts to bring that contemporary and authentic richness to our students in our classrooms.

MOVING INTO REAL-WORLD WRITING

The process writing movement of the 1970s, which continues to have positive effects in classrooms, is allied not to theory but to actual practice and, thus, to authenticity. The boldness of the research that Janet Emig did some fifty years ago is that she did not study how an Aristotelian or even a modern theory of rhetoric and writing could be enacted in students' writing instruction. For Emig, and for those who have followed her, the central issue was *what real writers do when they write*. Breaking with what was at that time considered the standard, Emig actually watched what actual writers—in this case, high school seniors in New Jersey—did when they wrote. Thus was born the idea that writing is a messy, halting, and recursive process, not a neat deposit made into the account of a writer from some very full and very golden writing bank in the sky. The process made sense because it mirrored the actual practice, back and forth, of real writers. This is, in essence, the heart of authenticity, and when we move away from it to the inauthentic kinds of recipe writing instruction we often give students—*write an outline and then follow it; choose your topic sentence and then structure everything around it*—we deny the reality of what any student or adult writer knows about how actual writing processes work.

Being honest, authentic about writing processes is a vital first step for students and for their teachers. How we actually produce writing is vital to honest discussion of craft, revision, and value.

A second step in authentic writing that is also vital is the writing itself. Some decades ago, a funny and smart English teacher named Ken Macrorie satirized what he saw being produced in English classrooms—not English as we know it, but what Macrorie termed *Engfish*, that false language and artificial prose that is suitable only for teacher and student consumption. It is, truly, not a fault or blame situation, but when we ask students to write about school-based topics over which they have far less command than do their teacher-readers, they often try to match what we require by writing inauthentic, stilted prose that usually puts the student writer in some sort of phony position and voice: *In today's society . . . ; A third reason why . . . ; In conclusion, I have told you that . . .*

The student writing generated by school-based topics—such as *why a bond issue is vital; how/if video games negatively affect young people's minds; why college should be a goal for every-one*—becomes part of this false equation. On the other hand, student writing may not be so stilted when it's put in the service of topics that have more appeal and even more prima facie validity, such as *why I should be able in school to send texts anytime anyplace; why using a Juul is not the same as smoking.*

In language and education, adherence to the inauthentic can also be a barrier to relevance and result in certain standards and rules being applied in inappropriate situations. Leila recalls an incident from her school community in Virginia.

IN THE SMALL CITY *where I taught high school, the local newspaper reported on a school board meeting at which one of the board members raised what was, for him, a highly disturbing issue. The previous week he had been at an all-school athletic banquet honoring the coaches and athletes who had distinguished themselves in the regional championships. The event was held in one of the high school's cafeterias, where students, parents, and community supporters also attended to honor the athletes. Standing in line for the buffet, moving toward the meatloaf and fried chicken, the school board member reported, he overheard two student athletes chatting to each other. He was appalled, he observed, at their language—it was full of incomplete sentences, slang, distorted pronunciation, and rambling observations. The incident*

so disturbed him that he brought it up at the board meeting with the observation that if this was what the English teachers were teaching students, then something was seriously awry in education. His observations were covered fully by the local paper and resulted in a number of letters to the editor, op-eds, and some public testimony from the school personnel in charge of English instruction. At no time, however, did anyone question why the entire issue was totally bogus. Considering context, audience, and message, the blissfully unaware athletes were doing exactly what their English teachers would have understood: communicating clearly with each other in context, aware of audience and accomplishing a defined purpose.

How is it that we as the English teaching community so consistently fail to make this message stick? How is it we miss the mark by failing to remind our public about the limits—and indeed the history—of correctness, of tailoring language to purpose? Of expressing, in context, valuable ideas?

Unless educators take a broader view of language and language use, our writing instruction will be stagnant. We want to engage our students in powerful, real writing that engages with the world beyond school. So what can a conscientious veteran teacher do to be authentic, to be a better teacher of writing and to be more open to how language actually functions in the world? We can start with a realistic model of writing processes (not a singular, lockstep *the* writing process) that includes the culminating step of writing in the real world. This step is too often left out of classroom writing: publication.

A WRITING PROCESSES MODEL: POWER-P

Real-world writing takes creativity, organization, strategic planning, discipline, confidence, enthusiasm, skill with language, and a thick skin.[1] We can't really teach all these qualities;

however, we can design authentic writing experiences that will allow students to develop these qualities over time. Ken uses the POWER-P acronym to describe the authentic writing processes he engages his students in (see Figure 2.1).

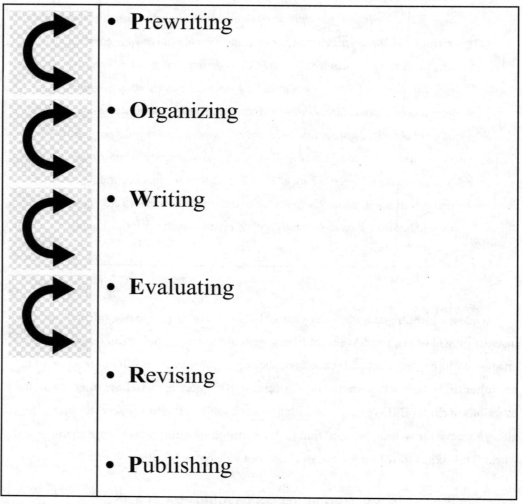

- **Prewriting**
- **Organizing**
- **Writing**
- **Evaluating**
- **Revising**
- **Publishing**

FIGURE 2.1. Steps in POWER-P.

As the arrows in Figure 2.1 represent, real writers move recursively through the many components of writing processes, and, in fact, different writers use difference processes at different times. Thus there is no such thing as THE writing process but, rather, many processes that writers may use to compose. We must caution again that a writing processes approach is *not* a lockstep recipe for writing or writing instruction. Using the POWER-P acronym that way could result in extremely *inauthentic* writing, and that is the last thing we mean to suggest. As veteran teachers, we can incorporate POWER-P in instruction and use it as only part of a comprehensively authentic writing instruction.

Teaching students about the many options they have for composing is an authentic approach and one that we recommend. Different components require writers to focus on different aspects of writing:

> **Prewriting:** Also known as the rhetorical concept of "invention," prewriting is when writers develop ideas they can write about, exigencies or changes they believe should be made in the world around them. There are many strategies for prewriting, including webbing; brainstorming; drawing; talking with peers; using various graphic organizers; freewriting; outlining; reading mentor texts; reading Twitter, Instagram, or Facebook feeds; reading local newspapers; and conducting specific internet searches. Often this component in a writing processes approach is given short shrift. Encourage your students to take the time needed to develop an idea they truly care about. The more time students spend thinking about how they can approach their topic and what kinds of evidence, rhetorical appeals, sources, stories, and other elements they can use in their writing, the more likely they are to be invested in the writing and successful in their final product.

> **Organizing:** Organizing is when a writer begins to decide how the piece of writing will be structured. What parts will come first, second, and so on? When will different forms of evidence or anecdotes be used? How will it end? Strategies for organizing include outlining, cutting out printed paragraphs and sentences of freewriting and moving them around, making a list, and following the structure of a mentor

text. Often writers find gaps when they organize their writing, and they return to some prewriting strategies to fill in those gaps.

Writing: This is when writers write a complete first draft. They take notes, sketches, phrases, outlines, and whatever else they've so far created and write them up into a draft that takes whatever shape is appropriate for the assignment. Again, gaps may become apparent, or the purpose of the writing may take a turn to the more specific or more broad, or a student may find a point of nuance not recognized earlier that requires more focus. Also, the student may return to previous components of writing processes. And, of course, some of the prewritten and organized material may go directly into the writing as well. These need not be entirely separate steps.

Evaluating: Once a writer's purpose is clear and a complete draft is written, much of the work is still ahead, as you well know. Successful writers work hard to reflect carefully on how effective their drafts are and to find areas that can be improved. To evaluate their writing effectively, writers can read their drafts carefully; ask peers or writing tutors to read their drafts and make suggestions; read their drafts out loud to themselves (or have a computer read it to them); run a draft past a test audience to see if the draft does what the writer intends it to do; and more. This is a crucial area that is often under-attended to in English classes. Let the name of this stage remind you why you should take it seriously: eVALUating. This is a point at which students can truly take their writing to the next level—and if they've written a piece about which they truly care, they will want to make the effort to do so.

Revising: Once writers make decisions about what's working well and what could be done better in their drafts, they make revisions to improve them. This is often an ideal time for peer response groups, as peers can be helpful in finding areas in the writing that are not entirely clear or not authentically engaging to an audience. Peers can point out areas that need improvement even if they can't make the perfect suggestions for making those improvements, and those areas can become worthwhile challenges for writers. Peers can also help writers solve draft problems that the writers already know about. Powerful peer response discussions can begin with a writer saying something like, "I know some people get confused by this sentence, but I need help making it clearer." Revisions often include major organizational shifts, deleting and replacing whole paragraphs and other changes. Other revisions will include surface corrections and minor tweaks that would be properly called "copyediting." (Note that it doesn't make sense to do any copyediting until the major revisions have been made. Once the draft is close to its final form, though, copyediting and proofreading are essential.)

Publishing: Finally, the writing is published. Too much school writing is all dressed up with no place to go. Real writing is always published in some form, and there are many, many forms of publication writing can take. In a traditional classroom, publishing is turning in a final paper for a grade. This is the weakest, least engaging, and most artificial form of "publication." Unfortunately, it is also the most common form in English classes. Instead, publication of writing can include:

▸ Being printed in a school newspaper, national journal, trade magazine, or some other print forum read by an audience outside the class

▸ Being posted online on a personal, school-sponsored, or professional blog or website, tweeted out to followers, or sent to friends on Facebook, Instagram, Tumblr, etc.

▸ Being read out loud to a real audience (that audience can be the whole class, a group of peers, or a school event to which the whole neighborhood has been invited)

▸ Being delivered to an intended audience who can take some action the writer desires

Real writing is always published in some meaningful form, and in most cases writers will get feedback from that audience (and we provide many more suggestions for publication in a subsequent chapter).

The implications of a writing processes approach are serious: We cannot spend Monday getting ideas, Tuesday writing, Wednesday revising, and Thursday editing. If we put students on such a schedule, even in the name of process writing, we are not letting students explore their own recursive processes. If we truly believe writing is recursive, we must create schedules that encourage recursiveness. This doesn't mean we abandon our students and give them three days to figure it out for themselves; we need to help them during this time by using a workshop format. In a processes model, however, we cannot completely confine writing behaviors to certain blocks of time—authentic writing doesn't work that way.

THE STARTLING POTENTIAL OF WRITING ON SOCIAL MEDIA

We are in an interesting time for writing in general. Social media is reaching new levels of prominence, and as a result, little-known authors can suddenly be thrust into the spotlight and have greater impact than would have been thought possible just a few years ago. Our colleague Jennifer Ansbach knows this feeling well, as a tweet she wrote on February 18, 2018, in response to reactions to a school shooting went viral (see Figure 2.2; @JenAnsbach). The tweet included an insight Ansbach had about the role of dystopian literature in the increasingly effective leadership of young people on social media. Among others, Beth Reynolds was inspired by Ansbach's tweet, and she even used it to make a sign for the March 2018 #MarchForOurLives protest she participated in (@wren_beth). The tweet became a physical sign in a political and civic demonstration, blasting the genre of a tweet far past its original boundaries.

We asked Jennifer Ansbach if she would share with us what the experience of garnering such sudden attention was like. A veteran English teacher and author of a terrific new book, *Take Charge of Your Teaching Evaluation*, she agreed to spend some time in our ideal Teachers' Lounge.

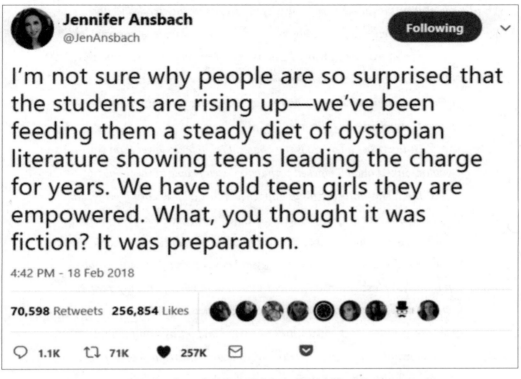

Jennifer Ansbach
@JenAnsbach

Following ⌄

I'm not sure why people are so surprised that the students are rising up—we've been feeding them a steady diet of dystopian literature showing teens leading the charge for years. We have told teen girls they are empowered. What, you thought it was fiction? It was preparation.

4:42 PM - 18 Feb 2018

70,598 Retweets **256,854** Likes

💬 1.1K   🔁 71K   ❤️ 257K   ✉️   ⌄

FIGURE 2.2. Jennifer Ansbach's tweet about the impact of literature on teens.

───── FROM THE TEACHERS' LOUNGE ─────

A Teacher's Tweet Heard Round the World

Jennifer Ansbach
Manchester Township High School, Manchester Township, New Jersey

In the aftermath of the Parkland, Florida, shooting, I watched as people who seemed to be out of touch with American public schools began to comment on how scary the view is from the floor (seemingly unaware that this is something

*our students are used to because we practice active shooter drills), and
how the students seemed ready to rise up en masse against a government
they believed was not putting them first. I tweeted about these responses
all weekend, and then one tweet went viral. More than 250,000 likes,
more than 70,000 retweets—and many people in my mentions. In the
process, I realized a few things.*

*Did I attract a few trolls? Of course. Probably far fewer than you
would think, though. I blocked perhaps a dozen people in the following
week. But a few fantastic things happened. I met a lot of caring people in
my mentions too: people who were genuinely surprised by my comments
and thanked me for pointing out what they hadn't considered; people
who took the time to read through several days of my tweets and engage
in thoughtful discussion; a teacher from Canada who shared my Twitter
stream with her students and allowed me to talk to them further and hear
some of their feedback; invitations to appear on podcasts and submit
essays (including this one) and do interviews and mention people in my
tweets, to make some people feel seen and included.*

*Now, I prepared for this in some ways. I had published a book a
few months before that tweet. I had already been posting on blogs and
having a lot of conversations, so there were people who already knew my
name, and I had about 3,400 followers (and 90,000 tweets at the time my
response tweet went viral—overnight success takes a long time). I gained
an additional 3,000 followers in the days following that tweet. Perhaps
that's what people should take away from this. For too long, teachers have
been told to go to their classrooms, shut the door, shut their mouths about
policy and education, and teach the children. However, by thoughtfully
and strategically engaging in a larger conversation over time, I had set
myself up for the opportunities that came my way.*

Take the risk. Share your authentic self. Speak passionately about things you are passionate about. Educators need to take back the narrative of education, to be part of the discourse and not just the subject of it. Put yourself out there regularly, and one day, when you least expect it, your words will resonate with like-minded people, and the community that helps you grow will grow too.

The world of education is vast, but your voice matters. Model for your students what engaged citizenship looks like and open yourself up to new possibilities.

Whether we always want to acknowledge it or not, real-world writing is shifting and expanding. The rules of engagement continue to change. If we as writing teachers don't adapt and stretch, we risk becoming increasingly irrelevant as teachers of genuinely useful knowledge and skills. So, as veteran teachers, we embrace the real-world of writing and pronounce it an exciting time, a time to be out in front and to help our students make the most of the writing opportunities before them. And let's remember: We teachers are not out there on our own. Organizations such as the National Council of Teachers of English (NCTE) publish useful research and policy documents and advocate continuously for those of us who keep our classrooms relevant. Let's look at one such important document.

NCTE'S *PROFESSIONAL KNOWLEDGE FOR THE TEACHING OF WRITING*

In 2016, NCTE passed a position statement listing and explaining what writing teachers should know. A lengthy and useful guide, founded on principles of authentic language instruction, NCTE's *Professional Knowledge for the Teaching of Writing* underpins much of what is highlighted throughout this book. The main points of the statement—and we concur with all of them—are the following:

▸ Writing grows out of many purposes.

▶ Writing is embedded in complex social relationships and their appropriate languages.

▶ Composing occurs in different modalities and technologies.

▶ Conventions of finished and edited texts are an important dimension of the relationship between writers and readers.

▶ Everyone has the capacity to write; writing can be taught; and teachers can help students become better writers.

▶ Writing is a process.

▶ Writing is a tool for thinking.

▶ Writing has a complex relationship to talk.

▶ Writing and reading are related.

▶ Assessment of writing involves complex, informed human judgment.

When we first started teaching and learned more and more about our students and about the literacies and forms of literacy around us, we realized that language and writing are anything but simple. Even the subheadings from NCTE's position statement reveal some of that complexity, and we invite you to read the entire document: http://www2.ncte.org/statement/teaching-writing/.

CONCLUSION: *RELEVANCE* AND *AUTHENTICITY* AS OUR WATCHWORDS

There is a lot to consider in the teaching of writing. It's a tremendously complex and interesting activity that cannot be easily grasped, stabilized, and explored. Like some taxidermied animal, the moment we capture writing—as soon as we take it from its natural home as a moving object between author and reader—it can become stilted, dead, artificial. Working with living language is as challenging as holding a wriggling fish with wet hands, and the temptation is to club the writing, as the fish, stopping its movement so we can see what makes it alive, and then teaching our students to "do that." Countless writing curricula are available that will assist you in teaching Engfish, dead writing based on artificial genres and antiquated rules that Edgar H. Schuster once called "[r]ules that do not rule" (47). You won't find that here.

Instead, we believe writing instruction should be based on two things: relevance and authenticity. Teaching writing this way is without question more difficult, but we believe that you as a veteran teacher are up to it. It requires letting go of some old shibboleths, acknowledging that students may have important things to say, and that it's not only okay but also important that we and our students take real risks in writing. Doing so will make the journey we call teaching more valuable and, certainly, more engaging and more fun.

CHAPTER 3

Writing in the Real World: Authentic Writing Assignments

Communication in the real world is complex, multifaceted, and messy. It is challenged by power, position, and prestige. It is subject to critical thought, social context, and personal assumptions. Communication changes based on the communicator, the reason for communication, the audience for the communication, and the means of the communication.

The only way students will experience real written communication and come to understand all the nuances of language and the social dynamics involved is to engage in *authentic* writing: real writing, written for a real audience, for a real purpose, in a real forum.

Let's now look at the creation of authentic writing assignments that will engage our students (and we their teachers) in the kind of writing that speaks to real audiences and is subject to all the genuine messiness and guesswork that is part of real-world communication.

AUTHENTIC WRITING: TWO EXAMPLES

Here's an out-of-the-mouths-of-babes example: Students in Constantine Christopulos's second-grade class at William V. Wright Elementary School in Las Vegas, Nevada, were unhappy with the mushy string beans they were served too often at lunch. Inspired by the book *Frindle,* in which a young boy's quest for change catches global fire (and a book you should read, if you haven't already), the students considered a boycott of the cafeteria. Their teacher suggested instead that a letter writing campaign might be more respectful and have greater impact. The students agreed and wrote letters to the lunchroom manager, asking for a change in the menu. Given the quotes from the students' letters in a widely reprinted Associated Press news story (Nakashima), it seems clear that Mr. Christopulos must have worked with the students on their letter writing rhetoric.

For example, the students included praise of the other food in their letters ("The food is so yummy and yummy. But there are one problem. [sic] It is the green beans." "We love the rest but we hate the green beans."), and the letters were exceedingly polite. The success of the students' campaign was tangible and relatively swift: The students were rewarded with a tasting of all the available vegetables to choose from, and the lunch staff promised more variety with considerably less reliance on green beans.

This was very likely one of the most powerful writing experiences these students had ever had. They wanted change (they had what rhetorician Lloyd Bitzer calls an "exigence"), they determined who had the power to make that change, and they communicated effectively in writing to convince that power player to make the change they wanted. All the pieces were there for an authentic rhetorical situation (see NCTE, "Rhetorical"), and the students were personally invested in it. In second grade, these writers made a real difference in their world that mattered to them.

As we are writing this book, a far more serious controversy than what's for lunch has developed and has engendered an extraordinary set of communications about social change. These have been published mostly on social media and fueled by the high school students of Marjory Stoneman Douglas High School in Parkland, Florida, where an armed student killed seventeen people on February 14, 2018. The surviving Douglas High School students have met with members of the national and Florida State Congresses, inspired rallies and many news articles and television media events, and even sparked two national protests: a nationwide school walkout on March 14, 2018, and a March for Our Lives protest on March 24, 2018. The student leaders from the high school have become celebrities for their work and are networking with other students from subsequent school shooting locales (such as

Santa Fe High School in Texas). These young people are quickly amassing recognition and hundreds of thousands of Twitter followers, and one of them is seriously considering a run for the US House of Representatives. These are seventeen- and eighteen-year-olds making national news with their rhetoric and their challenge to gun rights advocates and the tenets of the National Rifle Association.

One particularly interesting communication is a Douglas High School student's response to a video statement produced by Dana Loesch, radio talk show host and gun rights advocate. Loesch's video is a challenging statement meant to shore up support for unfettered firearm access and put those who would attempt to erode it on notice ("Dana Loesch"). Sarah Chadwick, one of the Douglas High School student leaders, created a low-budget parody (@Sarahchadwickk) of the Loesch statement that works as biting satire; a compilation of the two videos (*Sun Sentinel*) makes the parody clear. Chadwick's work earned at least as much media attention as Loesch's expensively produced video.

Whatever your own response to the issue is, think about what this student work shows: with simple equipment and a little time, a high school student was able to compose, produce, and publish a parody video that has had national impact. This fact has not been lost on adults. An interesting article in *The Atlantic* (Wong) explores the ways in which the Douglas High School students were prepared through their school's curriculum to be effective in their advocacy; the students gained experience in their courses in journalism and theater, along with the research skills they developed in AP English. The *Atlantic* article also—importantly—points out that these kinds of courses are frequently unavailable in high-poverty schools, an inequitable situation we should all be aware of and that we should all work to put right.

We have demonstrated that there is great potential for authentic writing in schools and that young people can engage effectively in authentic rhetorical situations. And yet, what Grant Wiggins said about the state of writing instruction may be as true now as it was when he wrote it about ten years ago: "The point of writing is to have something to say and to make a difference in saying it. Rarely, however, is impact the focus in writing instruction in English class" ("Real World" 29).

We as veteran teachers can and should do better than this. We can create more assignments that allow students to engage in real-world communication, to forward agendas that actually matter to them, and we can help them complete those projects well, learn from them, and build lasting, portable writing skills that will assist them in their futures lives as writers. Writing Project Director Tim Dewar puts it well: "Our challenge is to teach our student writers that writing is this amazingly powerful tool for shaping the self and the world" (n.p.).

WHAT IS AN AUTHENTIC WRITING ASSIGNMENT?

In an authentic writing assignment, students write to a real audience for a real purpose in a real forum; but what does that really mean? An authentic assignment is part of a rich writing curriculum in which the students have a say in what they are writing and in which they dive deeply into all aspects of writing processes, from idea generation to revision based on empirical (real-world) feedback to publication. Students are then writing to an audience that has the power to take some kind of action the writer wishes them to take. If that real audience takes the action, then the writing was authentically successful. If not, then the writing was not authentically successful (but students can learn very well from authentic failure too).

In another book, *Making the Journey*, we included a chart for our readers that is presented here in Figure 3.1 and may be instructive regarding the difference between traditional writing instruction and the kind of authentic writing instruction we advocate. If you spend a moment looking at this chart, you will see that authentic writing instruction opens up the full processes of writing, creating spaces for students to compose, critique, think through the perspectives of specific audiences, try things out, evaluate how well their drafts work, revise, and then compose a final version for some form of publication. This is the kind of writing process we advocate. It is certainly consistent with what Ken and his students did some years ago.

	Traditional Model	Authentic Writing
Topic	Teacher determined	Teacher and student or student determined
Prewriting	Limited or none	Extensive
Time	Limited	Extensive
Help/Collaboration	None	Extensive
Response	From teacher only	From teacher and peers and audience
Response	Summative	Formative and summative
Revision	Limited	Extensive
Audience	Teacher only	Teacher and others, including audiences outside class
Structure	Provided by teacher	Provided by student and determined by nature of project
Genre	Primarily academic essay	Varies widely

FIGURE 3.1. Traditional versus authentic writing instruction (Christenbury and Lindblom, *Making* 300).

 **I ONCE TAUGHT A** *writing class in which the entire curriculum consisted of developing an online book/ website for public distribution on the internet. The book,* Improving Academic Writing: A Guide for Teachers and Students, *was aimed at high school through college students and teachers. For this project, we—yes, I wrote for it too—interviewed students and teachers to ask them what they might want to learn about. Then we thought about how long our audience would be willing to read and what kind of information they would want. In our online book, we made liberal use of bullet points and images and charts to generate reader interest. We asked readers in our target audience to read and respond to our drafts so that we could make changes and improvements. Some of those readers were members*

of our class and others were outsiders who volunteered to give feedback. In the end, we had a great assortment of 500- to 800-word articles on the topic, such as "How to Get an A in College Writing"; "What If I Have No Idea What to Write?"; "What Do Teachers Look for in Student Writing?"; "Using Humor to Disarm and Surprise Your Audience."

For the final project, we included an About the Authors page with a set of bios. (One member of class didn't want her work available publicly, so we kept her final works off the site once it went public.) I collected signed release forms from all the other students, just as with real writers— because they were *real writers! We also included a link for anonymous feedback so we could hear from anyone in the world who read our work and had a response. This was well before blogs became so easy to publish (check out wordpress.com, for example), but we did get some good feedback, and I asked some local teacher friends to introduce their students to the ebook/site.*

This project was exciting for all of us—for the students and for me as the teacher—because we had real readers we wanted to help, and we wanted to make sure the book/website was something we could be truly proud of. We solicited feedback from our real audience, which served as empirical data, and we used it to revise our work. As the teacher, I created reader response sheets, and I graded students on how well they made use of the feedback they received. Finally, we held lots of writing conferences to help us think through the feedback, get new ideas, and make an excellent product. I also built a lot of metacognition into the class, obligating students to reflect on their experiences and decisions as writers. That reflection was important to ensure the students would incorporate the experiences into their knowledge base, so they would develop them into portable skills that would serve them well later.

As an added benefit, for several years this collaborative work lived on the internet and was read and appreciated by real readers.

Ken's class engaged in a lengthy project that was both the content and the means of the course curriculum. But authentic assignments can be much simpler: a review on TripAdvisor, short articles for the school blog, a book review on Goodreads or abookandahug.com, a review of anything on Yelp, or a letter of complaint to just about any business establishment. The point isn't to create one complicated authentic assignment; it's to create a rich writing curriculum.

Grant Wiggins suggests two questions that can help us focus on designing authentic learning experiences for students:

1. Is the student regularly required to achieve a real-world result, appropriate to context, as a consequence of writing, and learn from the result/feedback?

2. Is the student regularly required to write for specific and varied audiences, so that studying and coming to empathize with that audience is a part of the assignment? ("Real World" 33)

If you create a writing curriculum about which you can answer *yes* to the questions above, you've got it right.

And there is a real benefit. Today, authentic writing is definitely popular. Two years ago, Ken wrote a blog post for *Teachers, Profs, Parents: Writers Who Care*, a site and blog sponsored by the Conference on English Education (CEE), an NCTE group. His post "Is Your Child Getting a Good Writing Education? Four Questions to Ask Your Child" has gotten close to 10,000 hits and has been shared more than 3,000 times on Facebook. His questions suggest that students should be writing in many genres, choosing their own topics, writing to audiences other than the teacher, and getting feedback from real audiences other than the teacher. Another post, "School Writing vs. Authentic Writing," also received thousands of hits. It focuses on the real-world skills students can get from authentic writing instruction, such as:

▸ analyzing audiences;

▸ writing in formal and informal registers;

- ▸ analyzing and understanding the different conventions required for different genres (such as letters to the editor, business report summaries, and blog posts);

- ▸ and, writing for practice audiences (or peers) to see how real readers will react to their writing before they release it to the world. (Lindblom, "School" 2016)

Now let's hear from another teacher who finds blogs a great way to engage students in real-world writing, including writing scripts for video. When Evelyn T. Pineiro tried having her seventh-grade students compose video blogs (or vlogs), she found that the experiment paid off.

─── **FROM THE TEACHERS' LOUNGE** ───

The New Writer's Notebooks

Evelyn T. Pineiro
Oceanside Middle School, Oceanside, New York

"You have the period to write." Usually those words were followed by a forty-five-minute parade of students back and forth to my desk, but for the first time, not a single child asked me what to write about or how to start. We had just spent a week in my seventh-grade English class exploring different blogs, designing our own, and brainstorming topics. Elena was doing a DIY blog, John a humorous tour of the galaxy, Thomas a blog on life hacks, and Brooke a baking site.

All of a sudden, school was starting to intersect with the world they knew, one made up of vloggers who regularly recounted to millions of viewers around the world their morning routines, arguments with parents, or even panic attacks. Today's students know the innermost thoughts of strangers, and they are eager to have a platform to share their own. In some ways, they understand the concept of audience better than we do. Everything is public for them on YouTube and Instagram.

But if we teachers are not going to shake things up, kids are going to write the same lifeless drivel they think we want—"How I Spent My Summer Vacation." So we have to start by exploring powerful examples of voice in writing. Doing this begins to free students from the hard-and-fast "writing rules" they are ready to outgrow. You mean, I can use *I* in my writing? And begin sentences with *and?*

Now they aren't just students turning in assignments for the teacher to grade—they are writers who have their own styles and loyal readers. And this ownership of their craft transfers to the other writing they do. Students start to understand how to change their diction depending on who their audience is. They start to experiment with different styles and forms, realizing that most writing is not organized around "three reasons why. . . ." They start to see writing as a way to put their voices out into the world and, maybe for the first time, be heard.

STUDENTS' AUTONOMY AND AGENCY AS WRITERS

Authentic writing requires an author who is writing about something he or she knows and cares about, at least to some important degree. Asking students to write about traditional and standard topics, such as imagery in a literary work or a summary of an article on the death penalty, is unlikely to motivate enthusiastic writing, unless the student is already personally connected to those topics in some way.

Essentially, it's important that students have the opportunity to choose what they write about and that they are able to write from a position of expertise. That doesn't mean students shouldn't have to do any research, but the research is most authentic (and best done) when students are researching topics of interest and within (or at least near) their comfort zones. It's worth repeating that *only in school are writers expected to write for an audience who usually knows more about the subject than they do.* In many ways, that's a bizarre and somewhat impossible rhetorical situation.

Alison Marchetti and Rebekah O'Dell acknowledge this in their recently published *Beyond Literary Analysis: Teaching Students to Write with Passion and Authority about Any Text*: "Something wonderful happens," they say, "when we stop putting all our energy into teaching the symbolism in *Heart of Darkness* just so students can write about the themes of the novel" (26). Instead, they suggest, we should ask students to write about something they are interested in, and for good reason: "[W]hen students write from their passions and expertise, they can focus on mastering those tools instead of trying to simultaneously learn and master content" (27).

Maisha T. Winn and Latrise P. Johnson advocate for authentic writing instruction within a framework of culturally relevant pedagogy, which, they compellingly argue, brings students' "right now" to the classroom (31). They describe how a veteran teacher, Ms. Jane, shifted her planned unit on persuasive writing to align it with a local controversy that had engaged her students. A brother of one of the students had been recently harassed by police, and he and other students were "visibly shaken" by it (28). Ms. Jane refocused her unit on this topic, "demonstrat[ing] that, even in a standards and test-driven climate, it was not only possible but necessary to find authentic writing tasks that motivated her students" (29). Ms. Jane brought in relevant readings on police brutality and attempts to address it, allowed ample discussion for students to share their experiences and ideas, and then the students followed up in writing on discussion board posts.

Focusing on students' real lives, including social and political situations, doesn't just interest students more in an assignment; it also allows them to "access personal experiences and engage with multiple texts" as they undertake that assignment (Winn and Johnson 33). Focusing on students' "right now" helps to develop their sense of autonomy and agency as writers.

Following are some ideas for other personal topics (developed from suggestions we detail in *Making the Journey*) students could write about for a real audience:

- **Scars:** Leila picked up this assignment from a National Writing Project colleague. Students tell the story of how they received a scar. The student could turn it into a cautionary tale or an essay about the event. This assignment made Ken think of a burn he has on his arm from his days working at McDonalds; he could turn that experience into an essay on workplace safety for teens (including research into the federal Occupational Safety and Health Administration), or a confessional essay for his blog about adolescent carelessness and maturity. Or he could use the burn scar to compose a melancholy soliloquy designed to convince his spouse to treat him to his favorite dinner, assuaging the sadness and anxiety brought on by his sudden recollection of this adolescent trauma. (Hey, she knew what she was getting into!)

▸ **Quotations:** Students can select a quote that is meaningful to them and compose a tweet or meme for others about what it inspires in them, including a link to relevant websites, or even their own blog.

▸ **Childhood memories:** Young students remember many aspects of their childhood that they'll one day forget. Allow them to use their memories to write letters to their relatives or to compose an essay that might be appropriate for a trade magazine or website (check out the annual *Writer's Market*) or even a class website that other students will read and comment on.

▸ **Daily news:** Ask your students to scroll through daily news feeds or websites and bring in articles of interest to them and use the articles to spark ideas and issues they care about. They can develop writing project ideas to make a positive change on the matter.

▸ **Local issues:** Is there a park that should be cleaned up? A store that needs support? A local business that is needed? A person who should be recognized? A safety issue that should be addressed? Students can create public service announcements on video and/or in writing to raise the alarm in local communities and incite change. (See Esposito for some excellent models.)

▸ **Games, movies, music, books:** Do you have recommendations to make to other adolescents? Have you played a game that you must share? Has a book touched you so deeply that you want to write a blog post about it?

These ideas are just places for students to start. Students will need encouragement, advice, and guidance as they explore their own interests and devise ways to get their ideas out to real audiences. That's where veteran teachers come in. We can help students with all of that. And we can use curriculum standards, library and librarian resources, advice from colleagues, and collaboration with other classes to increase our own efforts.

It's also the case that writing in the real world is sometimes full of the pressures of on-demand writing and writing to please others, not just to influence them. Leila's brief period as a full-time professional writer still resonates with her today.

 **IT'S A CONVOLUTED AND** *not necessarily happy story, but for four years I actually left teaching and worked solely as a writer and editor. This was not a great time in my life, but I made the best of it. I also learned a great deal about making a living by writing. This was something that, with all my academic degrees and teaching exper-tise, I had never had to face. What did I learn in my real world of writing?*

First, I learned that timed and on-demand writing is not confined to school-based activities and high-stakes tests. I had to generate press releases and reports in a matter of days, if not hours. These tasks were not completely routine, but my ability to quickly churn out something respect-able was indeed part of my job. And I did it.

Second, other eyes and feedback were essential to my success as a writer. With the kind of quick writing I occasionally had to do, as well as with the longer pieces, having other people read—and often brutally edit or revise—my work was not something that occurred only in a fairy tale version of writing. It was part and parcel of how I succeeded.

Third, in my writing work, mistakes in facts and inaccurate phras-ing were not seen as mild boo-boos. They could be the basis for losing a raise, losing a professional reputation, or losing a job. In my office setting as a writer, I watched bad things happen to people's careers when writing was not sufficiently vetted or checked. This was not a happy lesson to learn, but it was effective and truly focused my professionalism and precision.

Fourth, I learned that regardless of your own writing talent and linguistic bent, you wrote within limits and to the specified audience. In one of the scariest writing assignments I was given, I interviewed our CEO, and the final piece, if accepted, was slated for wide publication. The CEO was not warm and friendly but well known for her demanding and contentious nature, and when she finally signed off on the copy (which I had rigorously edited, massaged, and yet attempted to make sound like her), I was incredibly relieved. At the end, she also gave me her version of a real-world writing compliment when she told me directly that she did not at first think I would be able to do this assignment successfully, yet I had. Thanks. I guess.

MORE IDEAS FOR AUTHENTIC WRITING ASSIGNMENTS FROM INSIDE TEACHERS' CLASSROOMS

Where can we look for additional authentic writing assignment ideas? *English Journal* and other NCTE sources are great places to find examples of authentic writing projects. Here are a selected few.

THE GREEN FOOTPRINT PROJECT

One of our favorite articles concerns the Green Footprint Project, in which Kim-Marie Cortez-Riggio has her middle school students work in groups to create and distribute pamphlets and give presentations to local community members about serious environmental issues in their neighborhood. Cortez-Riggio worked with educators in science, math, and social studies to infuse the projects throughout the curriculum, and she organized events with real community members in attendance. The Green Footprint Project had great impact on the students' sense of themselves because they determined their own projects and got their views out into the community: the students as writers and social change agents "became more aware of their existence in a larger world and perhaps they even became more aware of their future life purposes" (Cortez-Riggio 42–43).

PREGNANT AND PARENTING TEENS TALK BACK

In another excellent *English Journal* article, Heidi L. Hallman writes about a class of pregnant and parenting teens who were personally offended by a letter to the editor of their local paper describing the program they were in as "enabling students in making poor choices in their lives" (43). The students' teacher, Bob Schaefer, used the occasion of the letter to guide the students in responding to a real-world context responsibly and professionally.

Schaefer dedicated the next several classes to assisting the students with their responses, and a week later a powerful letter to the editor by the students appeared in the same paper. The students expressed their own empowerment and were gratified and surprised that their letter was published.

Hallman's account is also powerful because, as a professor of English education, she unpacks in depth how the experiences Schaefer undertook with his students allowed them "to make and support claims that are complex and multidimensional. Through the process of crafting their letter, they were able to position themselves in dialogue with [the original letter writer] as well as in dialogue with societal views concerning teen motherhood" (47).

BLACK STUDENTS PROMOTE MORE ACCURATE REPRESENTATION

Similar to Hallman, Tom Rademacher, 2014 Minnesota Teacher of the Year and English teacher and author, also had a group of students respond to an article in his local paper. Rademacher's original thought was to have the students analyze two recent articles about students in the state: one article was about students in a mostly White, affluent school, describing students as being underserved by low expectations. The other article, written in the same week, was about a mostly Black school, describing students as "inherently violent and scary" who needed "taming." A student in Rademacher's class said, "Oh, hell no," and suggested, "We need to do something" (*It Won't Be Easy* 155). Rademacher adds:

> Not learn something, not complete something, do something. Do. So they did.
> . . . [T]hey were going to spend the hour working together to draw attention to
> the racist garbage in front of them and push a narrative of young Black kids that
> reflected them much better. (155)

Rademacher's students put together an action plan and spent the day tweeting to and about the offending author and the article, using the author's own ill-informed words against her. Although that wasn't his plan for the class, he let the students follow their passion. In the end, the students' work "entirely fulfilled the purpose of the original [assignment]," which was to have the students engage in study of articles to discuss word choice and other devices used by the authors to make a point (156).

COMMUNITY PROFILES

Occasionally newspapers will pick up on a school assignment that has an impact beyond the classroom. For example, Megan Moore, a middle school teacher in Burke, Vermont, was featured in her local newspaper (Nixon, "Students Create"), in a story that was then picked up by *U.S. News & World Report* (Nixon, "School Project"), for having her students create twenty-six profiles of local community members. Students interviewed their subjects and their subjects' parents, former teachers, and others at length. They then wrote profiles in class and even created linoleum block prints of their subjects in art class. All the work was displayed publicly in a local cafe, where real patrons perused the gallery. The show was called "Humans of Burke."

The students' work was clearly inspired, judging by some profile excerpts:

- ▸ "During the summer Eric Bogie can most often be seen in the hay fields of Rye-gate and Danville area. The hot July sun beating down on him, his wife and two kids as they heave the fifty pound bales up onto a large trailer to bring home to their horses, cows and goats. The stench of sweat lingers in the air as the kids heave bales up to their father who stacks them perfectly so they don't fall off the trailer when they drive home." —Aiden Bogie

▸ "Have you ever felt safe because of just one smile, laugh, or just a look? Well this is how Tracie Surridge has made many students, club members, and others feel. She is that type of person who you know cares. Surridge is a committed mother, wife, teacher, and leader of a group called Modern Woodmen of America (MWA)." —Brittany Webber

WATER SAFETY FOR CHILDREN AT THE BEACH

Ken's local newspaper occasionally highlights good work done by local teens. In March an article highlighted a high school student who created a series of informational pamphlets about water safety for children who visit Long Island, New York, beaches (Ebert). The information was distributed to local surf clubs, boys and girls clubs, and lifeguard programs. While the student composed these pamphlets for her Girl Scout Gold Award, this is also the kind of authentic writing that could easily fuel an English class.

SCHOOL-INSTITUTED MOMENTS OF SILENCE

Illinois English teacher Elizabeth Kahn used the institution of a new "moment of silence" law in her school to inspire students' writing. Kahn didn't think to do this until she heard students talking with one another about it with interest. At first, the situation became an exigency for research, and the students asked: *What is the point of a moment of silence? How does the new regulation read?* The question *Is a moment even enough to make a difference?* led to an empirical study of the lengths of the moments of silence over the course of a week.

Kahn gave her students the choice of writing a letter to the editor or a letter to a state legislator explaining their view on the issue. In the end, the class was divided evenly over the value of the new law. Along the way, students engaged deeply in the activities of authentic writing:

This situation provided a great opportunity for students to learn effective strategies for writing an argument: taking a position, analyzing their audience, finding specific supporting evidence for their claims, analyzing the evidence, and anticipating and addressing counter-arguments. (15)

Student interest may not always serendipitously fall into our laps, as it did in this case, but Kahn believes (and we agree) that teachers can usually find similar controversial situations in which students will quickly become engaged (16).

AUDIO PODCASTING

Audio podcasting is another genre to consider incorporating into your classes. Sticking to audio allows more focus on the composition of words and organization of ideas, rather than video, which also requires careful attention to myriad visual details. Podcasts can be just a couple of minutes long and still offer useful information.

For example, *Merriam-Webster's Online Dictionary* often includes a brief *Word of the Day* podcast. Here's one on the term *nuance*: https://bit.ly/2Lijkp6. How about having students create short podcasts about terms in a class novel you've read? The next year's students could access those podcasts and write brief comments or notes of thanks to the previous students.

IDEAS FROM TWITTER

Twitter and other social media outlets are also great places to find excellent suggestions for authentic writing assignments. The tweet in Figure 3.2 from Scott Zukowski, an instructor at Stony Brook University, is about a writing project in which his students wrote Twitter posts for the Long Island Museum to publicize an upcoming exhibit (@scott_zukowski). This is an ingenious way to engage students in history and in contemporary written communication.

Scott Zukowski
@scott_zukowski

Following ∨

This past semester, my students served as experiential learners at the @LIMuseum and turned their extensive archival research into 280 character posts for the museum's Twitter. Check it out! #teaching #sbu

Long Island Museum @LIMuseum
LIM collaborated with @EGLStonyBrook on a William Sidney Mount inspired endeavor. In honor of the new Mount exhibition, Perfect Harmony, opening February 16th, the students posts will be released throughout the month of February. #monthofMount ...

1:28 PM - 2 Feb 2018

FIGURE 3.2. Scott Zukowski's tweet about his students' Twitter-centric authentic writing activity.

AUTHENTIC WRITING ASSIGNMENTS BASED ON THE WORKPLACE

Think also about the kinds of writing that goes on in real workplaces. This is the kind of writing that most students will need to produce effectively for the rest of their lives. In an excellent blog post, "Writing in the Work World," Ann D. David, Dorothy Meiburg Weller, and Amber Funderburgh describe a workshop they designed to engage participants in workplace writing. To prepare for it, they polled their friends to see what kinds of writing they did in their work. The types of writing their friends listed offered "an amazing range" (n.p.):

- ▸ A press release about an upcoming concert

- ▸ Photographs and captions

- ▸ Speeches to trade organizations

- ▶ Computer coding

- ▶ Diagrams

- ▶ Client/patient progress reports

- ▶ Emails, including discussions of manufacturing specifications and quotes for customers

- ▶ Email conversations with supervisors

- ▶ A contest essay

- ▶ Scientific reports

- ▶ Field notes

- ▶ A redacted police report

- ▶ Charts

- ▶ A graph about soil samples made by a geologist

Consider having *your* students complete some of these genres. Better yet, have them explore the kinds of writing that adults they know, as well as adults in the community, engage in at their workplaces (see Leila's story on p. 41) and ask the students to write presentations about them and share examples. Such a unit would offer countless opportunities for authentic writing assignments about authentic writing.

Anyone who's been teaching secondary English knows the work of Jim Burke, a gifted teacher and almost impossibly productive author. His *The English Teacher's Companion* is a must-read, and his *What's the Big Idea? Question-Driven Units to Motivate Reading, Writing, and Thinking* is one of our favorite books in the profession. But you don't have to attend one of his standing-room-only NCTE sessions to hear some advice from him, because Jim has stepped into our Teachers' Lounge for a few minutes, taking a break from his demanding day. Jim has a complementary take on what constitutes an authentic assignment: for him, bringing workplace genres into his classroom is a great way to engage students in authentic writing.

─── FROM THE TEACHERS' LOUNGE ───

Bring the Real World into Our Classrooms

Jim Burke

Burlingame High School, Burlingame, California

Instead of designing authentic writing assignments that my seniors send out into the real world, I find myself designing writing assignments for my seniors that reflect the forms, features, and functions they are sure to encounter *in the real world. What do I mean? What does this look like in my classroom?*

It means that students write a formal proposal, based on my careful study of proposals from the real world, in which they lay out the case for their major research project topic and subsequent approach to investigating it.

It means that after they have done most of their research on this major research project, my students write an executive summary based on a professionally designed template I adapted into a Google Doc that requires them to think about the form, features, and function of the executive summary as a document (goo.gl/Zk3713).

It means that instead of having seniors write a more traditional essay in which they outline what they will do after graduation, I require them to write a personal business plan using a template I adapted from the Small Business Administration's online resources. Thus, instead of narrating what they will do, they make an argument as to what they want to achieve and why those achievements themselves warrant investment for the reasons they outline in their business plan.

These real-world forms have in common the core thinking and writing moves that our students need to know for the more traditional

49

writing assignments we also design. I suppose what I am admitting here is that lately I find it difficult to make the connections with real-world people and organizations I used to, due largely to the loss of the woman in our school's career center who helped me make and manage those connections. Instead, I do my best to compensate by bringing into my class the types of writing those people in the real world have taught me matter. It is these more authentic writing assignments that help us prepare our students not just for college and their careers, but also for their lives as citizens and consumers who must be able to make a living and make a life for themselves.

WHEN YOU DON'T HAVE A REAL AUDIENCE: PSEUDO-AUTHENTIC WRITING ASSIGNMENTS

It may not be possible or even necessary for every writing assignment to occur in an authentic rhetorical situation, with a real audience, in a real context, and with real consequences. But that doesn't mean the same principles and some benefits of authentic writing assignments can't apply. Ken coined the concept (and term) *pseudo-authentic writing* in a 2004 *English Journal* column, "Writing for Real." In such situations, students write as themselves to imagined audiences or as imagined authors to themselves or other imagined audiences. And, in this case, the *pseudo-authentic* term is not meant negatively; it is an attempt to accurately describe writing that uses the imagined, not the real. Pseudo-authentic assignments can be truly helpful because they can approximate an authentic writing situation and raise valuable discussion.

For example, if your class is reading *Romeo and Juliet*, consider having the students write a letter from the Friar or Juliet's nurse beseeching the parents of the young lovers to let them marry. To turn up the rhetorical heat a bit more, have other students in the class answer those letters as the parents.

Or have your students write a letter from Steve Harmon from Walter Dean Myers's *Monster* explaining to his younger brother how he got caught up in criminal activity. Have other students write from the perspective of other characters in the novel (the prosecutor, the defense attorney, the other defendants, the shop owner who was killed) to Steve, and then ask the students who wrote as Steve to write back.

Ken was inspired to create such assignments by Judith Barlow, a professor of drama at the University of Albany, while he was earning a master's degree there in the late 1980s. Professor Barlow's take-home final exam required the students to write letters from one playwright the class had studied to another, citing specific aspects of the specified plays; it was a brilliant way to engage the students deeply in creative synthesis and evaluation of the works.

Moving from writing in response to drama and novels to writing in response to nonfiction, Joel M. Freedman created an innovative approach that also teaches empathy. Freedman had his students read a *New York Times* article about a young gay man who was murdered in a hate crime. The article included quotes or statements from about twenty people connected to the event. Freedman designed writing assignments that required his students to write a letter, article, sermon, proposal, or request about the killing from the perspective of any of the people in the article. If you wish to use this kind of "frame" for a writing assignment and make this pseudo-authentic, the students could be asked to aim their writing at a specific audience. Other students could be asked to respond to that writing as the imagined audience to which the original students were writing.

James Fallows and Deborah Fallows, an *Atlantic* reporter and a linguist, respectively, recently published an account of their five years of visits to little-known American small to medium-sized towns. In *Our Towns: A 100,000-Mile Journey into the Heart of America,* they frequently comment on the schools they encounter, and they were impressed with what we would call the pseudo-authentic approach one teacher took to writing.

At Camden County High School, a teacher, Rich Gamble, teaches writing based on his work as a former Naval Criminal Investigative Service (NCIS) professional. Gamble's students conduct forensic crime scene investigations (of manufactured crime scenes) and write up notes, reports, and court testimony, all following the standards for those genres, such as the requirement for very concise writing for the courts. It is, for this veteran teacher, a success: Gamble said that the student writing ends up as high in quality as the writing he saw as an NCIS investigator.

When the real audiences students write for are professional audiences, students are also learning about the kinds of work available to them and how writing skills factor in. For examples of other workplace genres to teach, see David, Weller, and Funderburgh's *Writers Who Care* blog post. Examples abound, and we believe that teaching authentic workplace genres can be highly motivating and provide a context for excellent real-world discussions about writing.

CONCLUSION: BRINGING THE ENERGY

Bringing in the real world through authentic writing assignments and shaking up your literary study with pseudo-authentic writing can deliver a bolt of energy into your classes. We veteran teachers know that engaged students are so much easier to teach. Even better, students motivated by their own interests can be far more eager to learn and to work hard.

We also know that authentic writing requires a bit more up-front planning time from us as teachers, and that when we engage in it we also take a bit of a risk, especially if this is new for a school community. But the payoff for you—and, most important, for your students' future—is well worth it, and it opens up the world of school into the world.

Promises and Perils of Advanced Authentic Writing Instruction

Authentic writing instruction is an advanced approach to teaching, and one that we believe should be used with students of all ages and abilities. Bringing student writers into the real world of writing creates greatly enhanced opportunities and can truly set fire to students' engagement, creativity, and empowerment.

Bringing students' writing into the real world also increases the opportunity for real consequences, both positive and negative. If we are serious about using authentic writing in our classrooms and with our students, we need to pay attention to the potential controversies and issues that can arise. While this is no reason to shy away from using authentic writing instruction, we would be less than candid if we did not outline, for you as a veteran teacher, the kinds of challenges (perils) as well as the truly rewarding aspects (promises) of bringing into your teaching authentic writing instruction. In this chapter, we examine both, beginning with the promises.

TRIANGULATION AND REFLECTION

An excellent advanced writing analysis that one can do well only with an authentic or pseudo-authentic assignment—that is, an assignment with a specific real or imagined audience—is triangulation. Veteran teachers already know that students don't learn from experience alone; they learn from their own reflections, or metacognition, about their experiences. It is in this reflection that students assimilate new knowledge into their previous knowledge base. This assimilation allows students to access more knowledge in the future, expanding their expertise.

This is truly promising and truly good news. Expertise is portable. If students have rich, authentic writing experiences and reflect on them effectively, the skills they develop will transfer to their future writing experiences. Triangulation enables deep reflection on authentic writing.

Let's look deeper at triangulation.

Using *Romeo and Juliet* as our text, imagine that a group of students is asked to write a letter to Juliet's parents from the Friar and another letter from Juliet's nurse, both of whom aim to convince Juliet's parents to allow her to marry Romeo. The Friar and the Nurse would have different evidence to marshal, different tones of voice and registers to command, and different characters (or ethos) to exploit. In writing the letters, students would have to consider the differences, but they might not be that mindful of them until they performed a triangulating reflection. Figure 4.1 is a visual representation of the triangulation. In this case, the letter authors are triangulated, and students would be asked to analyze the differences between the letters written to the same audience for the same purpose by two different people. This kind of analysis would engage the students in deep study of the rhetorical appeals and other devices used by the different authors.

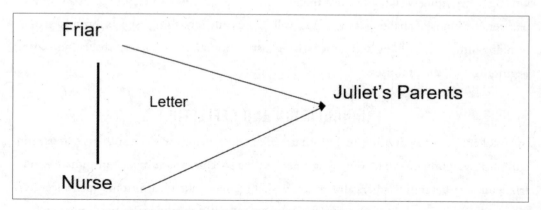

FIGURE 4.1. Triangulation reflection of characters from *Romeo and Juliet.*

It's also possible to triangulate other aspects of writing. For example, if students were asked to write one letter from the Friar to Juliet's parents and another letter from the Friar to Romeo's parents, some of the rhetorical devices might be the same, since they are coming from the same author, but that author might employ his rhetoric differently: use different evidence, change his tone, make use of different forms of his own character, raise different points (see Figure 4.2). After all, the Montagues and Capulets are different families with somewhat different interests, and their children are of different genders. In writing to each family, the Friar might consider the family's heritage, their values, the concerns for a daughter versus those for a son, the economic and social and legal implications of the marriage for each family, the specific feelings each family might have about the other. What would be most convincing to the Montagues and what would be most convincing to the Capulets? All of these differences in content, tone, and rhetorical devices could make for rich reflection on how the Friar might write these different letters. If their teachers take the time to make these links in discussion with students, this reflection also opens students to more options they have as writers in their own rhetorical situations when they are writing as themselves.

It's also possible to triangulate genres, but for that we use a different example (see Figure 4.3). In this case, let's imagine students want their community to build a video game arena as part of the neighborhood center. Should they write a letter to the editor of a local paper or tweet a blog post out to the community? Or both?

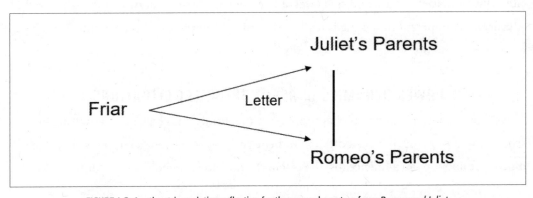

FIGURE 4.2. Another triangulation reflection for the same characters from *Romeo and Juliet*.

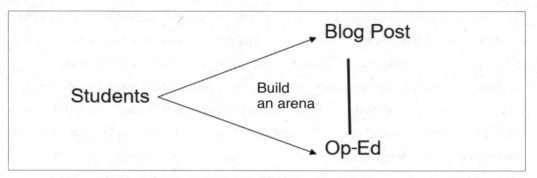

FIGURE 4.3. A triangulation reflection for writing genres.

Deep reflection on the differences between genres, audiences, and authors (and purposes, forums, and more) will give students significant experience and knowledge about writing. When students take this discussion seriously, their consideration will be complex because there are no certain conclusions. On the other hand, these are very much the kinds of thinking that go into writing in the real world.

One note: Please don't be fooled into thinking that triangulation is for advanced students only. It's not. Frankly, it's for advanced writing *teachers* of writers at any level. All writers can focus on rhetorical differences, especially if they are guided by a knowledgeable teacher who has set the stage for these high-level conversations about writing. Such conversations will help students develop advanced rhetorical skills they will be able to call on later. But no matter the age and skill level of the students or the expertise of the teacher, this advanced development in writing is really only available when students encounter authentic writing assignments.

POWER DYNAMICS IN REAL RHETORICAL SITUATIONS

As we have explored in previous chapters, one of the intractable challenges of writing in school is that our students most often find themselves writing about something they don't much care about to an audience (us, the teacher) who knows much more about the subject than they do. Only in school is this a common occurrence. In real-world writing, the author almost always knows more about the subject than the intended audience does. And the author cares about the subject and is looking for some specific action from the audience: support, agreement, cooperation, understanding, funding, a vote, a change in policy, a date, a permit. The list is endless. But another important aspect of real-world writing, and what we would highlight here, is that the power dynamic between the author and the intended audiences shifts depending on the rhetorical situation.

In a post on the *Writers Who Care* blog sponsored by NCTE's Conference on English Education (CEE), Ken (Lindblom, "Power Dynamics") identifies three kinds of rhetoric based on the power dynamic between the author and the audience:

- **Writing Up:** when a writer is writing to an audience with more power than she or he has

- **Writing Down:** when a writer is writing to an audience with less power than she or he has

- **Writing Across:** when a writer is writing to an audience with about the same power that she or he has

Writing in each of these situations requires writers to make careful decisions, to take into account the power level of their audience. Unless students are given authentic writing assignments, these are high-level rhetorical skills they will never have a chance to develop.

When students practice Writing Up, Writing Down, and Writing Across, they can also use a series of questions to help them think through the kinds of power dynamic they are facing in these different scenarios. Teacher Janet Neyer was engaged by Ken's post and his accompanying questions and created a handout that presents the questions in a visually appealing manner (see Figure 4.4). Neyer welcomes teachers' use of this handout, which is also available for download.

Know Your Audience!

Important questions to ask when writing UP:

- How much time is my audience likely to have? How can I reach them immediately and be sure my point is heard?
- What forms of evidence will convince my audience? Might they want statistics and/or expert testimony?
- What type of writing does my audience prefer? Have I written in a style that will appeal to them?
- Do I need to establish my credibility as the writer? Do I need to counter some preconceptions my audience has?
- Is the tone of my writing one that the audience will appreciate?
- Are the conventions in my paper up to the expectations of my audience?

Important questions to ask when writing DOWN:

- How does the audience feel about me?
- Have I made sure that my tone does not talk down to them and that it matches the content of my writing?
- How much detail must I use in explaining things to my audience? Will they understand my topic or will I need to work at making it clear?
- Have I addressed my audience in a way that is inclusive and thoughtful?
- Have I used vocabulary and conventions in a way that welcomes my audience to the conversation?

Important questions to ask when writing ACROSS:

- How can I convince my audience to care about my topic?
- What will grab their interest?
- Does my tone assure my audience that we are equal?
- Have I written in an informal tone?
- How can I create a sense of togetherness in my writing? Might I use we and us instead of I and my?
- Have I answered the "So-what?" question for my audience? Why does my writing or this topic matter?
- Have I used vocabulary and conventions that my peers will appreciate?

Adapted from Lindblom, Ken. "Power Dynamics: Writing Up, Writing Down, Writing Across." Blog Post. Teachers, Profs, Parents: Writers Who Care. 13 Feb. 2017. Web. 18 Feb. 2017. <https://writerswhocare.wordpress.com/2017/02/13/power-dynamics-writing-up-writing-down-writing-across/>.

FIGURE 4.4. Janet Neyer's handout of Ken's Writing Up, Writing Down, Writing Across power dynamic.

RHETORICAL CHOICES

Authentic writing in a variety of rhetorical situations—that is, writing for lots of real purposes, to real audiences, in real contexts—gives students the kind of experience that will help them write in many situations they will encounter in their lives outside school. If students focus most heavily on traditional school writing, they are likely to think that the best writing for school is the best writing for everywhere else. As we know, they will quickly find out in the world of work and the world of higher education, that's just not true.

Making the best rhetorical choices as a writer is complicated. The more experience students have with varied purposes and audiences, the better they'll be able to handle tricky situations when they arise. Effective writers are versatile and flexible; they understand shades of meaning and how those shades affect audiences. They write with nuance. They pay close attention to who their audiences are, and they make themselves aware of the power dynamics they are writing within.

Once again, these skills are not reserved for advanced writers, but are instead accessible to writers at any level. In fact, even young children employ quite sophisticated rhetorical strategies that account for power dynamics when they speak to their parents versus their peers when they want something.

▶ "Dad, I put my toys up. Now can I have a cookie?"

▶ "Angie, you're my younger sister, so you have to share your cookie with me."

Talented teachers with good, level-appropriate authentic assignments can engage any student in advanced rhetorical thinking.

Julia Torres, a high school teacher in Denver, Colorado, rightly sees authentic writing instruction and publication as empowering for students. Students in her class read culturally responsive young adult texts and then use them to support school and community engagement with their own texts. Torres has made a stop in our Teachers' Lounge, where she explains.

FROM THE TEACHERS' LOUNGE

Empowering Students through Publication

Julia Torres

Montbello High School, Denver, Colorado

I like to have students read a range of literature from across different cultures. I teach AP English Language and Composition and AP English Literature and Composition. Some of the texts we have read include Toni Morrison's The Bluest Eye, *Che Guevara's* The Motorcycle Diaries, *Jason Reynolds's* Long Way Down, *and Elizabeth Acevedo's* The Poet X. *I have not found these texts (especially the YA reads) to be typical choices for AP English classes, due to the misconception that the texts aren't complex enough or the language elevated enough. I believe this is an oversimplification of the genre, as there are so many different texts underneath the umbrella of "YA." We are in a renaissance of sorts for culturally relevant YA that deals with pertinent sociopolitical issues.*

Reading these texts, inviting the authors into the classroom via Google Hangouts, watching video interviews from them, and reading their tweets, other creative endeavors such as poetry, and blog posts is a great way to build a bridge between the discourse we would like our students to participate in and the world they naturally inhabit. Students' lives include these other genres and conversations, and so should our classrooms.

With regard to authentic writing assignments, my students have written arguments that connect to various topics of interest and then posted them on Medium.com, which allows for easy sharing via social media. This gives students an authentic audience and lets them play with online publishing. My students and I have also created mini-posters when we studied activists and change agents from our past. Students used SoundCloud to create audio clips of themselves talking about people such as Audre Lorde and George Jackson. They then made QR codes that linked to their sound recordings. The final step was to post their mini-posters in physical spaces where the school and the community could share in their learning.

It is my belief that the more true to life students' reading and writing experiences are, the more liable they are to see our classroom as a microcosm of the larger world. I believe in empowering my students by giving them a place to voice their views, connecting the world to them via Twitter, Medium.com, a class blog, and a variety of other means of publication.

THE CHALLENGES OF AUTHENTIC ASSIGNMENTS AND HOW TO MANAGE THEM

Authentic assignments are real discourse, and as such they can have an impact outside the classroom, perhaps even outside the school. Accordingly, these assignments and this kind of writing have real consequences and can have promises but also perils.

Generally, authentic writing means the writing will have some real impact on the author's interests: a letter in reply, an offer of apology, a change in a policy, an agreement to meet, an appreciative audience who better understands something. All of this is positive. But when we engage students in real writing, sometimes there are also unexpected and unintended consequences. Sometimes those are just what we want: a local newspaper catches wind of the topic and writes a story, your school administrators are delighted by the positive publicity, you are given medals and raises, and you're . . . okay, well, that might be overstating it. But in all seriousness, authentic assignments can lead to enhanced relationships between the school and local community citizens, businesses, nonprofit agencies, and more. To be honest, however, there can also be negative consequences; it is not a given that things always go well.

Here's one real-life nightmare scenario. A teacher in upstate New York wanted to "get students out of their comfort zones and teach them to debate points that are against their ideological perspectives" (Levin n.p.; see also McMahon). Toward that end, the teacher came up with a creative, pseudo-authentic writing assignment in which the students were to write memos—all based on real historical events—from imaginary senior leaders to a large, imagined audience on a controversial plan.

In terms of authentic writing pedagogy and engagement, the assignment was well thought out. Unfortunately, the rhetorical situation the teacher chose was probably not. Taking the stance of Nazi leaders, the students were to write supporting or opposing the "Final Solution," the systematic genocide of millions of Jews and other people who didn't fit the evil Nazi ideal. Some students given this assignment were understandably uncomfortable, and they allegedly told the teacher and administrators about their concerns. The administrator supposedly provided an alternative assignment for students who requested it, but the original assignment wasn't retracted. The issue received major media coverage, and the state commissioner of education, somewhat bravely in our opinion, defended the assignment as an attempt to engage students in critical thinking.

More outrage followed. The Anne Frank Center tweeted a call for the firing of the teacher, the administrators, and the commissioner (@AnneFrankCenter). The commissioner quickly retreated from her original position and stated that the assignment was inappropriate. The teacher's name was not reported, and it's not clear what the fallout was for him or her (Levin; McMahon). Our take is that we appreciate the teacher's intention but agree that the context of the assignment was ill-advised.

Tenure, academic freedom, case law—all exist specifically to protect educators from suffering because of the political leanings of those around them. But the strength of those protections varies considerably from school to school, state to state, and court jurisdiction to court jurisdiction. Nevertheless, veteran teachers must create authentic writing assignments that engage students in real thinking and real action, and we can't allow fear of repercussions to stop us. That said, veteran teachers—especially in dialogue with their colleagues, administrators, and union reps (if you have them)—can temper possible problems. The nightmare scenario just described is exceedingly rare; in fact, its rarity is partially responsible for the media attention it received. But teachers must be mindful that real writing does have real consequences. Veteran teachers who present authentic writing assignments that are both thought-provoking and well considered will need courage, resilience, and confidence. They will also need, we think, common sense.

Here are some ways to ensure your authentic writing assignments won't go awry, and how to ensure you'll be ready if they do anyway:

- Make sure your assignments are **carefully aligned with the written goals** of your school's curriculum, your state ELA standards, and the NCTE/IRA Standards for the English Language Arts. The more closely your assignments align with documented standards, the firmer the ground you stand on if you must explain your assignments to anyone.

- If your assignments are reaching outside your classroom to other parts of the school, **consider discussing them with your department chair and principal**. Ensure they know what you are doing before they find out from someone else who might be unhappy about it, even for some unpredictable reason. This discussion is actually an authentic rhetorical situation for you: try to make this more about a professional informing a colleague than about an underling seeking permission. After all, teachers should be the professionals making the decisions about their students' learning (NCTE, "Rhetorical").

- If your assignments will reach outside the school building (*yes!*), it's a good idea to **make sure the superintendent or assistant superintendent for curriculum knows about it, assuming you've also mentioned it to your direct supervisors.** Often, when community members are taken aback by something school related, they complain to a school board member, who then immediately calls the superintendent. It's better if, instead of claiming ignorance, the superintendent can say, "Yes, we're aware of the work the teacher is engaging the students in. Here's what it's about. . . ."

▸ **Ask your students** about the assignment. Do they foresee any issues? Is there anything about it that makes them uncomfortable? Student discomfort doesn't mean a teacher should retract or even necessarily revise an assignment, but we should listen carefully to see if our students are sensing something we are not. After all, we tend to love our own assignments, right? We can be blind to their flaws and, in the rush of enthusiasm for an assignment, fail to use our own good common sense.

▸ **Make sure that your students get feedback** from some other students, and make sure you have a sense of what students are doing before they deliver any discourse beyond the classroom. You shouldn't be controlling, but a teacher should be aware and be ready to intervene or guide when necessary.

▸ **Consider when you want to assign controversial subject matter.** We hope it's obvious that we encourage and even expect you as a veteran teacher to engage with controversial subject matter, but we want you to do it in a way that makes you successful and empowered. In many districts, it can make a difference if the topic comes from the students rather than the teacher. Listen to the students to see if there's an issue they are already engaged in that they can raise in the classroom; then help them engage with it responsibly. This way, your agenda is influencing your students' ELA skills, not their politics.

▸ For more information, consult the first volume in the Continuing the Journey series (Christenbury and Lindblom). We discuss issues of politics throughout, but we address them particularly on pages 145–48.

When we are a little uneasy about a controversial assignment, we like to consult our colleagues about what they have done. So let's head over again to our ideal Teachers' Lounge. As a veteran English teacher at Patchogue-Medford High School, Alison McKeough has found success using authentic public service announcement (PSA) writing assignments to engage students in canonical literature that aligns with the contemporary discourse on and of the #MeToo movement and other gender-related issues. She's in the lounge now, talking about some of the results she's seen.

──── **FROM THE TEACHERS' LOUNGE** ────

Engaging Canonical Text through Authentic PSAs

Alison McKeough

Patchogue-Medford High School, Medford, New York

Canonical literature is not necessarily something high school students rip from their teachers' hands and devour in one sitting. There's a reason it's called "assigned reading." For the teacher willing to let his or her students communicate with the world outside the classroom, there are ways to make literature accessible and, dare I say, interesting to young readers.

Asking students to interact authentically with real audiences when it comes to the study of literature isn't always easy, but for the last few years I have been taking a break from tired graphic organizers and the like. Instead, here's something I've found success with: "Gender Roles and Representations in Literature—A Public Service Announcement (PSA)." For this assignment, I ask students to examine a particular character, characters, or gender role in a work of literature and then create an original PSA to advise audiences of what happens when the types of behaviors they have identified are accepted. I've found that students get deeply engaged in and even enjoy discussions of how the roles of men and women are represented in canonical texts.

Here are some examples using Scout Finch from To Kill a Mockingbird, *a character most people are familiar with before leaving high school. For this assignment, students are expected to work together to examine how gender roles are either reinforced or changed in this text. Students first have to come up with a real decision about the way Scout is portrayed and how that might have an impact on her understanding of*

65

the world around her. Then students need to come up with an idea for a PSA that warns, educates, or entertains the public from the perspective of the character. I expect students to decide what the purpose of their PSA is, and this will ultimately drive the script forward and support an appropriate tone.

The result: students have produced original PSAs (videos) on their phones, editing with free apps such as Splice, Filmmaker Pro, and iMovie and sharing on social media. Through our students, Scout has voiced many concerns:

▸ *She has encouraged parents to remain open-minded about their children's choices, especially if they don't cause harm to their child or others (a nod to the way Atticus doesn't scold Scout for preferring to play in overalls rather than dresses).*

▸ *She has educated parents about the warning signs of abuse and how to recognize when a woman may be in a toxic relationship (a reference to Mayella's relationship with her father).*

▸ *She has educated people about what happens when we allow racism to infiltrate our communities with lies, hate, and violence, and how that has a direct impact on children.*

Teachers, prepare to be amazed: students typically pull out all the stops for this assignment! When you think about the possibilities PSA assignments can inspire with both male and female characters, it's exciting.

CONCLUSION: DON'T PLAY IT SAFE

We started this chapter with a handy alliterative phrase, *promises and perils,* and we hope that we have illustrated both here. Using authentic writing with our students can enliven and even transform our teaching. The promise is genuine. But moving to the other possibility, peril, we have tried to offer realistic advice. We want to emphasize that using authentic writing assignments, even if they might take more time to create and vet and even if they might seem outside the norm, is utterly worth it. Playing it safe in our classrooms is not a viable long-term strategy for the accomplished veteran teacher; authentic writing assignments stretch our students, stretch ourselves, and are often rewarding far beyond what we might imagine.

Feeding Back: Responding to Student Writing

One of our major hurdles even as veteran teachers is the struggle to respond to our students' writing. We know they need significant feedback: our experience as teachers confirms this, and research tells us that writing to which there is no response is writing that may never improve. We also know, however, that significant response is often unsustainable. Time, stamina, and the demands of the other parts of our teaching lives can all interfere.

How do we frame this dilemma?

Imagine there's a big machine into which you can slide a list of all the work you do in one day. You slide in today's list. After some humming, pinging, and popping, out of the machine comes back your list with comments about all the things you did wrong that day and how you should have done them instead.

How would you feel looking at that list of all the work you'd done, only to receive in return an itemization of your failures? And how would you feel if, because you had no failings that day, the list came out untouched with no feedback at all? How often would you want to use this machine? How willing would you be to feed into it your most personal, risky, challenging work?

Now imagine you *are* that machine. You spend significant time analyzing lists of tasks to find errors and missteps. You read list after list, searching for problems, finding corrections to make, and spitting the list out—only to have to process yet another list. And, as you continue, you find that the lists get shorter and less complex, less interesting all the time. The mistakes and problems are the same time after time. How eager are you to read the next list? How interested are you to discover what set of tasks another person is up to?

If you can accept this macabre image of a list-commenting machine, you are probably reminded of the worst of our work responding to student writing. It can, in short, be uninspired, mind-numbingly dull, and laborious. It can even become its own perverse self-fulfilling prophecy of failure, the result of which encourages less and less creativity and risk and results in more lifeless writing with more problems in it. Leila well remembers this in her teaching.

ONE OF MY EARLY TEACHING *struggles was responding to student writing. Even after some years of being in the classroom, I felt the pressure to provide students with something important. Regardless of the quality of the writing, I believed I had to come up with something tangible, some suggestions for improvement, some ways that the writing could be strengthened. In hindsight, with one tenth-grade class, I know that my comments were both frequent and discouraging— for some students, there appeared to be nothing they could do right, that would be enough, that could not be improved—always improved!—by revision. Student anxiety seemed to mount, and I realized there was a mismatch of expectations: in this one class, the students felt they were doing decent writing, but I made clear, through my comments and suggestions, that wasn't the case. Yet I felt I was being a responsible writing teacher. Students handed in their writing; I critiqued it thoroughly and consistently. On some level, however, I was not comfortable with the way the class was going, and I was realizing what I was doing had little positive effect.*

It was a poor cycle of interactions between this class and myself, but at the time I was not able to see my way out of it.

The proverbial dope slap came straight my way when, in the midst of working with one of our class writing textbooks, which reproduced and analyzed sample student work, I found, word for word, one of the essays a student had just turned in and to which I had made my usual comments, many of which queried how the essay could be improved. The student essay submitted had received a "revise and resubmit." Problem was, that same plagiarized essay was showcased in the textbook as exemplary.

The student never challenged me on my comments (which is enough to make me believe in miracles), and I was so concerned about the implications—for me as a teacher—of the deception that I never confronted him. Rereading the essay in the text, I also became concerned for the student, wondering what in the world I was thinking when I insisted that the essay could be extensively improved. What kinds of standards was I holding my young writers to?! I thought long and hard about why a frustrated student would have resorted to the deception he did—and also contemplated how I could change my own writing response so that it was less punitive, less negative, and more inspiring.

So let's go back to our machine, but make an important alteration. This time, let's imagine the machine's purpose is not to find fault with the work slid into it; rather, the machine's job is to find the *best parts* of the work and to highlight those, describing why they work so well. The machine adds praise to the list and makes suggestions about how the strengths exhibited could be expanded, used elsewhere, or repeated to greater effect.

Now if you had access to this machine where you could feed in all the work you did on one day and see an analysis of all the things you did well and why those were good choices, how often would you use the machine?

If you *were* this machine, how would you like to see the new ideas attempted and the new risks taken by the workers you are analyzing? You would see the best strategies repeated each time, and you'd see new ones tried. When the new ones worked well, you'd see them again and again too. There would be expanded work and new ideas on each sheet slid before your eyes. Would you feel more energetic now, seeking out the positives and finding all the good stuff, than in your previous duty, when you were looking only for flaws and faults?

In his fascinating new book on communication, *If I Understood You, Would I Have This Look on My Face?*, actor, author, and visiting professor of journalism at Stony Brook University Alan Alda describes a relevant conversation he had with a high-powered business leader on motivating improved communication. Their discussion involved the very principle we point to here, that working from a positive perspective is much more likely to yield good results than focusing on flaws:

> [The CEO] told me he once worked under someone who was a very tough leader. As in, "Make a better presentation next time, or you're out." But in the company he runs now, he feels he gets better results if he starts by praising what they had been doing well and then urges them to bring their next presentation up to that level.
>
> This is not just softening the blow; it's keeping in mind what the other person is thinking and feeling. And it's enlisting them in the effort to move them to their best. Instead of saying, "You've done a bad thing; don't do it again," he's saying, "You've done really good things; do more." The first gives them a vision of failure they somehow have to avoid, while the second gives them a model of success to live up to. (69)

Teachers are not machines, and writing students aren't simply slipping their work into a slot to get feedback. However, sometimes it can feel this way. And it can be exhausting, boring, and even depressing on both sides. Some veteran teachers get into a rut with student writing. Others get so frustrated they leave the profession. Yet making sure students receive appropriate feedback on their writing is one of the most important jobs English teachers do.

How can we do this job in a way that is energizing, reasonable in its demands on our time, and effective for building students' writing skills? In short, can we create regular, do-able practices for significant yet sustainable response?

In the previous chapter, we focused on authentic writing assignments that engage students in real writing for real audiences with real purposes in real contexts. In the following chapter, we take up assessing and grading student writing to ensure that students get appropriate credit and an accurate sense of their writing's quality. But good assignment design and effective assessment don't alleviate writers' need for response, nor do they allow teachers to abdicate that responsibility. In this chapter, we look at how teachers can make sure that student writing receives thoughtful, helpful response in a reasonable amount of time.

WHAT IS RESPONSE TO STUDENT WRITING?

Before we explore how to respond to student writing, even veteran teachers like us would do well to think about *what* response is and what it's supposed to do for student writers. Responding is not grading or summative assessment; those are separate processes that teachers engage in. Response is the second half of a conversation begun by the writer.

Response IS:

- Giving writers a sense of how their writing is affecting a reader
- Showing the writer what the reader is enjoying or finding valuable
- Pointing out bright spots in the writing
- Asking writers legitimate questions about what they intend in the writing (Why is this information important to you here? How does this relate to your larger point?)
- Telling the writer what is confusing to the reader

Response is NOT:

- A grade
- Listing errors
- A statement phrased as a question (e.g., Wouldn't a comma be appropriate here?)
- Listing directives:
  - Use MLA format.
  - Fix this run-on sentence.
  - AWK!
- Editing a manuscript
- Demeaning or discouraging, even inadvertently

- Telling the writer what the reader would like to read more about
- Encouragement
- Giving the writer ideas about options for revision
- Challenging or agreeing with a writer's expressed opinions
- Suggesting resources for assistance with a goal in the writing
- Support
- Helping the writer see that the communication is under his or her control

- Telling the writer what you would have done if you were writing the paper
- Explaining rules to a writer
- Correction
- Taking over the job of the writer

Ellen Foley, a former high school English teacher, literacy coach, and reading specialist who is now earning a PhD, works with preservice English teachers, helping them learn to respond to students' writing artfully and effectively. To our great good fortune, Ellen is in our ideal Teachers' Lounge, and she's willing to share some of the good ideas she and her students have come up with.

─── FROM THE TEACHERS' LOUNGE ───

Gentle Reminders for Meaningful Feedback

Ellen Foley
Western Michigan University, Kalamazoo, Michigan

It's no secret that students crave what we all crave when we submit our ideas to another person: validation that the ideas are understood, questions and suggestions for clarification, encouragement, and, according to Grant Wiggins ("Seven Keys"), specific feedback on our efforts

to reach a goal. With all of these demands, it's no wonder that providing meaningful feedback is so difficult!

To simplify this task, my students, a dynamic group of preservice teachers, compiled a list of "gentle reminders" based on the research read in our methods course. Their list is valuable not only for new teachers, but perhaps even more so for those of us who have taught for a while:

Don't:

1. Provide feedback when you're frustrated or tired. Take a break. Each student deserves a fresh, positive perspective.

2. Wait to give feedback. Timely feedback is powerful; the sooner students get it, the more relevant it is.

3. Be the students' editor. Think of yourself as a guide, showing students potential paths to achieve the next goal of a piece.

4. Use technical jargon or abbreviations. Many students don't know what "FRAG" or "AWK" means, nor what to do with that information.

5. Be vague. Goodwin and Miller stress that vague feedback—even the most well-meaning "good job"—can result in destructive uncertainty (What was good?), decreased motivation (Good enough!), and diminished learning (I'm good—nothing to improve here!).

Do:

1. Read the whole piece before commenting on it. Novice writers often take time to develop an idea—be patient.

2. Read supportively and with empathy. Take the student's ideas and efforts seriously.

3. Consider using the "Praise, Question, and Wish" strategy (Slusher) as a template for maintaining consistency in responding to each student's writing.

4. *Comment on the paper's main ideas, details, evidence, and structure in your own words.*

5. *Ask questions of the author and comment on the effect the piece had on you. Be curious, not critical.*

When we keep in mind how difficult, intimidating, and import-ant writing is, we're likely to reply with grace and understanding. At its core, this list reminds teachers to do just that: respond to students' work compassionately.

Another helpful way to think about the purpose of response is to imagine a range like that shown below. At the left end is one possible approach to responding to student writing, an approach that assumes the reader is not in control of the writing. Only in a few circumstances is someone else totally in charge of another writer's writing. The English classroom can be one of these odd places. In those circumstances, a teacher's response may prescribe what the writer should do. In fact, you'll likely have seen descriptions of writing instruction that include "diagnosing" student writing, for which a resulting "prescription" makes perfect sense. That responder might correct errors and direct the writer to make certain changes. On the other end of this spectrum is an approach that offers one reader's experience of the writing and offers a set of questions and options for a writer.

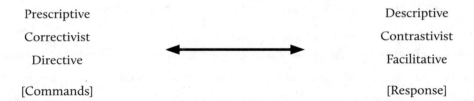

Prescriptive	Descriptive
Correctivist	Contrastivist
Directive	Facilitative
[Commands]	[Response]

Let's look at some approaches to responding to student writing. Here we draw on the terminology of Rebecca Wheeler, Nancy Sommers, and Lil Brannon and C. H. Knoblauch.

A **prescriptive** approach assumes one right way to write and enforces that way. A **descriptive** approach helps the writer understand how the writer's piece is only one possible way to write and helps that writer accurately assess the effectiveness of that way. A **correctivist** approach to student writing does a search and destroy for mistakes and errors. A **contrastivist** approach understands what the writer is trying to do and suggests options for finding more successful approaches in the specific case of a particular piece of writing, largely as a result of the audience and forum or genre. In sum, a **directive** approach tells student writers what to do. A **facilitative** approach asks writers questions about their writing, opens up the writer's thinking, and raises the possibility of other paths to take with the writing to enhance and increase revision.

Let's go back to the range we introduced on page 75.

Response is on the right side of the range, reinforcing students' sense of ownership of their writing, making them aware of the options they have as writers, and encouraging them to use the experience of an informed reader to their own advantage. If teachers tend toward the left side of the range in their responses to student writing—giving *commands*—they will disempower their students and discourage them from learning about the many options they have as writers. For sure, students may learn one way to write successfully, for example in a five-paragraph essay format, but at best it will be a gimmick, one specific form of writing they do well enough over and over again, like a one-trick pony. We have both had students who exhibit this; we're impressed with their first writing assignment, but then we notice that every subsequent submission is just another version of the same essay. For these students, writing is not a portable skill that will help them build success in other contexts outside school.

Responding on the right side of the range—giving *response*, not *commands*—generally requires a reader to comment knowledgeably about what writers do well. In fact, explaining to a writer what she or he is doing well is much more likely to stick with a student writer. Such a conversation is a welcome experience for students. And, because students are so open to learning in those moments, the new knowledge they build will be fully integrated into their knowledge base and made available as future knowledge for later situations. This is how portable writing skills develop. This is how writing expertise is built.

You can actually see this happen. Try it out. During a writing conference, say to a student, "Do you know what you did really badly in your writing?" You'll likely see expressions of concern and dismay cross the student's face, and his body language may convey an attitude of defense against the coming criticism. In another conference say, "Do you know what you did really well in your writing?" You'll see the opposite: the student's eyes will widen, and her chin will likely raise. She'll sit up in her chair and be open, even eager, to hear what you are about to say.

Many teachers may not focus on a lot of positive aspects of student writing because—honestly—they've never been asked to do so, or even thought to do so. But responses that concentrate solely on what needs to be *fixed* can inhibit, if not cripple, a student writer. Thomas Newkirk suggests in his most recent book that some teachers and students may "lack a vocabulary" about writing that can help students improve their writing (68), and we think that includes language about positive aspects of students' drafts. So, to address that concern, consider the following list of positive attributes that you might find in students' writing:

- Great voice. This really sounds like you.
- Such original phrasing.
- You describe the setting really well.
- Good use of a clever/useful title.
- Your ending is very satisfying.
- The ending wraps up the piece very well.
- This is very clearly put. Your readers will completely understand you.
- Adding this information is a good way to make the audience trust you more.
- Excellent first sentence. It really grabbed my attention.
- Your sentences vary in length, which makes your writing more interesting to read.
- This topic is really interesting.
- This is a very original thought.
- I think your readers will find this a very challenging idea.
- You followed the conventions of the forum in this case very well.

- Very effective use of deliberate sentence fragment, or run-on. (It's okay if the student didn't realize she or he was using these techniques. If the student wrote them, and they work, then the student gets credit for it.)

- Perfect place to end a paragraph/start a new paragraph.
- You took a risk as a writer here, and it paid off.
- I'm glad you used this sophisticated word even though you may not have known exactly how to spell it yet. That makes your sentence much more effective. Published authors do this all the time.

The point of focusing on the positive is not to ignore the negative aspects of student writing. It's to help students enjoy writing and to think of themselves as competent writers. Once students develop a sense of themselves as real writers with valuable things to say, they will be far more open to advice on how to say things in the best ways possible. That's when constructive criticism can have greater effect.

Blogger Patricia A. Dunn ("How to Promote") suggests good peer response can have several significant benefits, and we agree. It can:

▶ Help responders come to see the value of certain types of evidence or examples

▶ Help writers consider adding more details or needed evidence to their drafts

▶ Help writers see what's confusing to their readers while there's still time to revise

▶ Help writers see what's working, what in their draft moves or engages readers

▶ Help responders return to their own writing with a better sense of what is effective, or what to avoid

▶ Help instructors invest their time on more developed drafts

Anna J. Small Roseboro also writes blogs for English teachers, and in one post about peer response she lists several "values" of good peer response, including:

- Students get feedback from more than one source.

- Students see other papers that will be graded along with theirs, so they get a sense of the context.

- Teachers can scan drafts rather than making time-consuming responses to them.

TWO HELPFUL WAYS TO RESPOND TO STUDENT WRITING
SENTENCE STEMS FOR RESPONSE

Years ago Donald A. Daiker suggested a powerful and simple way to respond to student writing that still works well today. These sentence stems work especially well in early stages of the writing processes, and they are a great way to motivate students to expand their drafts while remaining empowered as writers:

- I like the way you . . .

- I'd like to learn more about . . .

These sentence stems focus the responder on the positive aspects of the writing and give writers suggestions for places to expand and enhance their text. And students are generally eager to receive responses like this. They know the responses won't be lists of their faults but will instead help them see the good in their writing and help them develop more of that. Daiker's sentence stems also work really well for peer response when you have students talk with each other about their drafts. (See much more on this below.)

FOCUS ON *PATTERNS* OF ERROR

If you are going to focus on correctness, which should always be toward the end of a student's writing process, it's important not to overwhelm the student with every minor problem. Students don't do well when the feedback they receive is a copyedited version of their writing. Making matters worse, the students who make the most errors are also the ones for whom the amount of error pointed out is likely to cause the most psychological damage, resulting in less confident, less fluent writing. In fact, research has made clear that if a teacher points out every error on every draft, two things happen:

1. Students write as few words as possible.

2. Students write in less sophisticated ways, choosing the safer strategy of using only simple sentence structure and a restricted vocabulary (words they are sure they know how to spell and use correctly).

Students are savvy, and if avoiding error is the most promising path to success in your classroom, they will take it.

But we can't avoid error entirely either. Students must develop the skills to write in ways that avoid errors. Ignoring error is an abdication of our responsibility as teachers. So what can we do?

Mina P. Shaughnessy, in her groundbreaking *Errors and Expectations*, suggests that teachers analyze student writing to find *patterns* of error. When a student makes the same error at least three times, it's not a mistake (or a typo); it's a misunderstanding of a rule. Those are the kinds of errors worth focusing on. So something worth considering as part of your response to students on later-stage drafts is looking for patterns of error and helping students learn the rule they are misunderstanding. These can include subject-verb agreement, misuse of apostrophes, inadvertent run-ons or comma splices—whatever patterns of error you find.

If you have trouble explaining particular rules, ask for advice from the ESL or ENL teachers in your district; they are very good at explaining the rules of standardized English. And, please, make sure you point students to a useful grammar and usage handbook so they can learn to look up rules as they need them. Using writing handbooks effectively is a skill students will take with them into the future. Finally, if you notice a student's error is misapplying a rule from another form of English—African American English (AAE), for example—be sure to teach the rules contrastively. AAE is not *wrong*; it is *different*. In cases where standardized English is required, the AAE rule doesn't fit, and vice versa.

Responding to student writing effectively is something all English teachers grapple with. So let's take a walk to our ideal Teachers' Lounge and see who's around. Great timing! Former middle school and prison program English teacher and now composition professor

Nancy Mack is there, working through a stack of her students' papers. She's got some good advice about what to keep in mind when responding to student writing, starting with the tone of our comments. Yes, writing comments on students' writing is its own challenging rhetorical situation!

─── FROM THE TEACHERS' LOUNGE ───

Feedback Should Support Teaching

Nancy Mack
Wright State University, Dayton, Ohio

How teachers word comments designed to suggest improvements makes a big difference in the writer's attitude toward revision. Pronoun choice can become unintentionally confrontational. I had to stop myself from equating the student with the written effort by starting every comment with you. *Passive voice is less aggressive, as in "This essay needs a stronger opening" rather than "You need a stronger opening." Choosing to use* you *can be like taking a step closer to the reader. Taking a step back when delivering negatives may be helpful, whereas taking a step forward when giving praise can have more effect—for instance, "You made several good improvements from the last draft." Of course, the content of the comment can be offensive no matter which pronouns are used. Research indicates that specific comments are more effective than general comments. For example, the previous comments could include the names for concepts that have been taught in previous mini-lessons: "Adding an introduction can pique the reader's interest with a brief dramatic* **anecdote** *or alarming* **statistics***" or "Your* **listing thesis** *helps the reader to predict the order of the sections." Adding the term* reader *may also reinforce the rhetorical idea that the audience for writing is not always just*

the teacher. Additionally, larger revisions should offer the writer a choice of options, as in the case of adding an introduction.

A notion that revolutionized my commenting on student writing was that feedback on drafts is not teaching—instead, feedback should support teaching that has already occurred. Formative feedback needs to be tied directly to the preceding revision mini-lessons. So, when students are revising narratives, I teach mini-lessons about action, dialogue, sensory details, and inner thoughts. Each brief lesson starts with examples in a model or mentor text that students mark with colored pencils, one color for each concept. This activity is followed by time to add sticky notes to the current draft with new additions. I always ask for volunteers to share one of their improvements with the class to reinforce and celebrate the changes. If the concept is difficult, such as wording a thesis statement, we might even problem-solve a particular sentence or word choice as a class. Students are given out-of-class time to incorporate their sticky notes into their drafts and to add additional changes.

Teacher feedback is most useful when it follows in-class modeling and revision. I have discovered that I can give feedback quickly by highlighting the revised draft with colors (Mack, "Colorful"). I use a three-color highlighting feedback system: green for good, yellow for could be improved, and pink for a problem area that needs revision. I limit the highlighting to only the concepts that we worked on in class—in this case, action, dialogue, sensory details, and inner thoughts. The number of concepts depends on two factors: the difficulty of the concepts and the time I have for giving feedback. I also insert brief positive reminders following the highlighting that name the concept needed: "Opportunity for more details about the action" or "Opportunity for dialogue." Using the word opportunity *in comments puts a more positive spin on revision. Highlighting can be done electronically on the computer or manually on paper drafts. Students say that the colors help them to know exactly where they need to revise.*

Nancy Mack has published some excellent works on responding to student writing. For more information about teaching and responding to students' narrative and other genres of writing, see her *Engaging Writers with Multigenre Research Projects.* If, like many other writing teachers, you're intrigued by Mack's use of colored pencils or computer highlighting for revision, check out her article "Colorful Revision: Color-Coded Comments Connected to Instruction."

PEER RESPONSE

For some teachers, allowing or encouraging students to read and respond to each other's work seems ultimately fruitless. They conclude that many students are uncomfortable tackling the work of response, especially if the draft is weak or unfocused, and many students avoid their uncertainty by using the occasion to socialize or do other work. This all-too-common experience should not, we think, lead you to move away from peer response. The key is student preparation and reinforcement.

Impediments to Constructive Peer Response

- Directions are unclear or inadequate.
- The responder is confused about the role and its responsibilities. (Should she or he correct spelling and grammar? Make suggestions for more writing? Point out confusion? Say what she or he likes? Point out deviations from the assignment requirements?)
- Responders and authors are skeptical about the real value of the response. (Won't the teacher just override the responder's suggestions anyway? Isn't getting advice from peers a waste of time if the teacher is going to assign the grade based on his or her own judgment?)
- Responders are asked to perform tasks above their current abilities (e.g., advanced editing and copyediting) and for which they haven't been properly prepared.
- Responders feel as though they aren't getting any credit for their labor.
- Peers have no idea what to say in their response.
- Responders don't want to offend their peers, so they offer nonspecific praise such as "This is good."
- Peers don't respect each other enough to give thoughtful, honest feedback.
- Writers haven't written something ready for a useful response.
- Students are apathetic; they simply don't feel like putting in the effort to respond or to take seriously the responses they receive.

Responding to a draft constructively is a high-level skill that, like every other sophisticated literacy skill, takes direct instruction, practice, and scaffolding. The good news is that when peer response is done well, it can exponentially improve the communication skills of both writer and responder, and it can significantly decrease the number of hours a teacher must spend responding directly to each draft of every student's writing.

In a post on the *Writers Who Care* blog, Adam Loretto, Sara DeMartino, and Amanda Godley offer excellent advice on making peer response work. They suggest that students get feedback from several other peers, not just one, and that getting contradictory advice is actually a positive because it "enabl[es] students to exercise authorial control and practice justifying writing decisions" (n.p.). They also recommend use of an anonymous, online peer review program, Peerceptiv.com, which they say can hold students more accountable for how seriously they respond to each other's writing.

We offer advice of our own on several important points for making peer response a valuable experience for all:

> **Providing adequate direction:** "Response," to students especially, is a confusing concept. Students need clear direction on how to appropriately respond to drafts of their peers' writing. In addition, it's often a good idea to model the process by putting a draft on a document camera or projecting it onto a whiteboard and responding to it together as a class. Use a paper with the name removed from a former student who has granted permission, or a "student" draft you have written yourself (to keep anyone from feeling put on the spot). In front of the entire class, model the kind of response you are looking for. In particular, students can be too eager to pounce on errors (just like some teachers), or they won't really know what they can respond to. You can give light guidance, such as using Daiker's sentence stems, or much more detailed directions, such as those presented in the handouts in Chapter 7. You might also give the students ideas for aspects of the writing to point to, such as the list we offered on pages 77–78.

> **Scaffolding and maintaining skills:** Response skills will wane quickly without practice, so it's important that students are given regular opportunities to read and

discuss each other's writing. Once a week is certainly not too frequent, but not all those peer response sessions need to be long. Incorporating peer response into quick daily writing is a good way to keep students' skills sharp without taking too much time. It's also important that peer response sheets are appropriate to students' developmental levels.

Ensuring the task is appropriate: We lament the fact that many teachers begin with peer editing, not peer response. Peer editing is probably the most difficult form of peer interaction about writing because of the psychological impact of focusing on error, coupled with sensitive peer dynamics. To make matters worse, most students are dreadful copy editors. In our experience, peers are as likely to point out stylistic differences as errors as they are to actually suggest changes that add error to student writing. The students find it unpleasant, the teachers find it unhelpful, and the practice of peer response in any form is quickly discarded. Too many times we've heard from otherwise well-meaning colleagues: "Peer response doesn't work." Instead of starting with peer editing (or ever assigning it), consider beginning with more open-ended responses and scaffold positivity and specificity. Again, Daiker's sentence stems are great starts. Give students lists of positive attributes they might point out, such as the list we offered earlier on pages 77–78. And they can just make marks in places where they are confused or want extra information. As students get better and better at this kind of response, it will become easier to introduce more constructive criticism and in-depth feedback.

Varying the modes of peer feedback: Consider using different modes for students to share feedback, making the process more interesting, helping students build new technological skills, and showing students many options they have as writers and responders:

- ▸ Writing on each other's papers, or copies of them

- ▸ Writing on Google Docs using Suggesting mode or in Word using Track Changes

▸ Having students speak face to face about their drafts, with the writer (or a designated recorder) taking notes—or use an audio recording device

▸ Giving oral comments via Google Docs or Word, both of which provide easy ways to do so

▸ Using Jing, Screencast-O-Matic, or other cloud-based, dynamic screen capture software to give feedback

Giving credit where credit is due: Since responding to a peer's text is itself an important literacy skill, and since it demands significant labor to do well, it's appropriate to assess students' work as responders and to give them credit for their response work in the form of grades, not just ephemerally as part of "class participation." Taking students' response work seriously will help students understand that you, as the teacher, value this effort and will encourage other students to also take it seriously. Assessing response work effectively will also help students improve their own literacy skills. Especially when it comes to written comments, it doesn't take too much time to evaluate students' peer responses. Even a simple rubric can help, such as the one in Figure 5.1.

	Well Done!	Okay	Keep Trying
The feedback is specific enough to be helpful for the writer's ideas for revision.	Targeted comments with specific sections cited	General comments with few specifics	General comments and no specifics
The feedback is respectful and positive in tone.	Praise offered, and suggestions are helpful and targeted	Little praise offered, and suggestions are made as directives	No praise offered, and suggestions are minimal
The feedback is focused on the areas required in the Peer Response Directions.	Feedback is clear, and most of the areas are addressed	Feedback is somewhat clear, but very few of the areas are addressed	Feedback is vague, and few or none of the areas are addressed
The amount of feedback is useful without being overwhelming.	Feedback is restricted to major areas of concern	Feedback covers almost every issue in the draft	Feedback is both vague and global

FIGURE 5.1. Peer response scoring guide.

Developing a community of writers/a culture of respect: Probably the most important ingredient of peer response (any response, really) is an atmosphere of trust. Both of us write a lot, and we have peers, including each other, whom we return to again and again for advice and criticism. To take people's writing seriously and to be truly open to other people's feedback requires caring about their opinions and trusting them not to be flippant, dishonest, or even abusive. A considerate, honest, productive community of writers doesn't emerge because a teacher tells the students to be one; it emerges because a teacher models and builds it with the students. That means starting off slowly with shorter, easier tasks, focusing on positive feedback, and then building toward more extensive writing tasks and giving constructive criticism and advice. Teachers must circulate the room, listening to conversations or otherwise monitoring the feedback students are giving each other, and they must consistently remind students of the value of the community they are building together. And, of course, if the teachers your students had before you have created writing communities in their classrooms, this process can move more quickly—as it can for the teachers after you. Throughout this section on peer response, we've included suggestions that will not only help in improving peer response, but also build a community of writers.

THE POWER OF THE WRITING GROUP

You might consider instituting static writing groups in your classes, in which the same students meet together for a period of time. It may be easier to create smaller communities of writers by having four to six students get to know one another and one another's writing strengths and weaknesses over the course of a number of assignments. The positives of this kind of approach are that your students may build richer, more sophisticated writerly relationships—in the best case, these relationships may even extend to writing outside your classroom. Clever teachers can build in assessment strategies that reward the entire group for any one individual writer's triumphs or improvements, leading to an even stronger sense of camaraderie within the groups. And friendly competitions among groups can also be established, as appropriate.

Of course, the power of the writing group depends on the ability and willingness of the participants, and, especially with adolescents, teachers must often step in to manage conflict or redirect off-task conversations. But if you think about it, the ability to manage conflict within a group, to be able to work with peers, and to be able to self-monitor are extremely important skills for adults to have mastered. Student writing groups can be great situations in which to develop these skills.

Ken often used static writing groups in his high school classes.

I REALLY ENJOY THE *human dynamics of group learning, and I used a lot of cooperative learning methods in my high school classes. With a new class, I would assign a few in-class writing prompts and a take-home writing assignment in the first week to give myself a sense of how each student wrote. Then I would put writing groups together with heterogeneous abilities and have them work together for at least a month, but often for a full quarter or more. To ensure the writing groups worked, I had to pay close attention to how they were going. I would walk around, occasionally sitting in on a group. I would ask the students to take a few minutes to write about how the group's work went that day. I would also meet once in a while with the full group and—most important—with each individual. In those meetings, I would learn about students who slacked off, about others who had significant writing challenges, and about the highly capable students who simply took over the group's work.*

That's when the most interesting aspects of the groups happened. I would design activities that required full participation by everyone. I would help students learn to convince each other to put in more effort. I would suggest methods to meeker students for speaking up to stronger personalities. I'd help those strong personalities relax a bit and let others have a say. In extreme cases—and let's be honest, aren't many situations with adolescents extreme?—I'd make private deals with students, promising them still high grades if they didn't do all the work for the group, or extra class participation points if I heard a student challenging a strong personality effectively. These kinds of private deals are often necessary to ensure that all students learn to their maximum capacity. They are the epitome of the saying, "Fair is not always equal." In the end, most of the writing groups worked well, and students learned from each other as well as from the mini-lectures and customized assignments I created based on my close knowledge of how the groups were working. Of course, some were flops. But that's what happens when you work with real people.

CONCLUSION: DISRUPTING THE MACHINE

Teaching, reading, and evaluating student writing can be a dull affair. At the beginning of this chapter, we asked you to imagine yourself as a machine responding dispassionately to writing. For most of us, unfortunately, that exercise in imagination probably doesn't take much effort. Meeting 100+ students multiple times each week can generate a lot of student writing, much of which can be routine and, frankly, boring. We need to disrupt the machine and yet provide our students with thoughtful and consistent response. How to do so on a regular basis requires creativity, positivity, and stamina—and these are just the kinds of qualities that are hallmarks of successful veteran teachers.

Significant Yet Sustainable Response: Handling the Paper Load

HELP FOR A TEACHER'S DILEMMA: FREQUENCY OF WRITING AND RESPONDING TO STUDENTS

If you can recall those first few years early in your teaching life, you may remember feeling that the English teaching enterprise might be rigged from the beginning, that it was an unwinnable game. Specifically, you might have felt that there were aspects of teaching you would never be able to resolve in the way you had hoped. You may have looked enviously at veteran teachers and their apparently calm work patterns and regular habits and, if you were fairly brave, you might have talked explicitly with them to ask how they did it. But the how-to-handle-the-paper load issue (and Leila actually contributed years ago to a book with that title [Stanford]) eludes most English teachers and is a source, for many of us, of real concern and even private anxiety.

Simply put, there is an unbridgeable gulf between how much students can and should generate in writing and what teachers can do in response. The heart of the matter, as every veteran English teacher knows, is not will or discipline but sheer numbers; when a teacher is responsible for 100 or more students and they create even a modest amount of writing every week, there is a huge inequality of time that cannot be easily bridged. Even a modest amount of writing generated can result in a workload headache. And for those beyond the early career jitters and all their nervous excitement and energy, the labor of responding to student writing can be downright exhausting. This is a major challenge—perhaps *the* major challenge—for even veteran English teachers.

THE CHALLENGE OF THE PAPER LOAD

Let's look at the practicalities. A modest two pages of writing a week from 100 students equals 200 pages of reading and response for a teacher. Even if those pages are given the most cursory and speediest attention (let's imagine under a minute to read, respond, and record the response to the two pages in some sort of record keeping), the response will take about three to three and a half hours. This is for only the least intensive response to one draft of student writing. Do the same count for a set of three- to five-page papers that require five to ten minutes of response each, and you're talking eight to seventeen hours of work.

These hours are, needless to say, on top of everything else you are doing: preparing for class, grading other assignments, meeting with parents, attending school functions.

Thus, the almost brutal reality of time to respond to student writing makes many veteran English teachers avoid regularly assigning much writing—they cannot read it all, and therefore it is not part of their daily work. No planning period can accommodate the consistent time commitment this writing demands, and the reaction from some teachers is simply to avoid it.

Yes, all of us know and see colleagues who are *never* without student papers. They bring them to athletic events; they pack them in their suitcases during weekend jaunts. Ken had a colleague who always had his "earthquake papers," which he carried everywhere, just in case he found himself with extra time: in a waiting room, on a delayed train, during a meeting at which he need pay only partial attention, or in a storm or other natural disaster. These teachers are continually working on responding to student papers; it is a constant in their lives. You may be one of those English teachers who is never without your stack of papers. If so, you are fighting the good fight and, of course, working under difficult circumstances.

But this is not feasible or sustainable for many English teachers, especially as we move through our careers and the demands outside the classroom become more serious and more time consuming. Veteran teachers with children, aging parents, and extensive community obligations are rarely able to give the kind of time to preparation and grading they may have envisioned and actually practiced early in their careers. Often their reaction and response is to avoid assigning writing frequently so that they don't set themselves up for the brute hours of work that such response seems to entail. Even with infrequent assigning of writing, many English teachers are woefully challenged to get papers back to students in a timely manner, struggling for days, if not weeks, to finish sets of papers.

Ken admits to spending days and days over the course of his career staring at stacks of papers, feeling guilt and shame as he avoided responding to them. Occasionally those papers would mutter, "Ken, you lazy bump! Stop sleeping, eating, dating—stop *living!*—and get back to work!" For the entirety of the four-hour round-trip drive to a prized annual arts festival, a carsick Leila once sat in the front seat of a friend's car madly grading research papers. It was grade the papers in the car on the trip or not go to the event at all.

And why do we go to these lengths? We know that when we take too long to get back to students about their writing, by the time the work is returned, its currency and even interest may well be diluted; after a few weeks, students forget what was assigned, forget their responses, and are not engaged in what a teacher has crafted. This was brought home to Leila just recently when an English teacher she visited ruefully noted that the papers her students had submitted well before winter break, early December, were, at the time of their meeting in mid-January, still untouched and not returned to students. Most of us, even if we don't admit it, have also been there—and too many times.

This is a rather melancholy situation, and it is for many teachers a source of private concern and even embarrassment or shame. It can be the kind of unpleasant little secret that we teachers keep to ourselves as part of what we know we have to do in order to survive. Almost every English teacher alive knows that students should be writing frequently, that writing often is the way to fluidity, competence, and confidence as a writer; but it is, in a real and human world, a challenge to even lightly assess that writing within the work parameters we are given.

This is not an optimal situation: students who write rarely write haltingly, and the quality of what they produce is often not what we want or expect. Writing frequently with some sort of check-in from a teacher is almost nonnegotiable; but when the only way to do this is to set oneself up for an unrealistic and burdensome workload, most teachers will quietly, and consistently, decline.

Massachusetts English teacher and recent Heinemann Fellow Kimberly N. Parker learned a valuable lesson from a veteran colleague about not giving too much of her time to grading. She's in our Teachers' Lounge, all ready to tell us about that important lesson.

— FROM THE TEACHERS' LOUNGE —

Don't Focus on the Writing, Focus on the Student

Kimberly N. Parker
Shady Hill School, Cambridge, Massachusetts

Years ago, one of my most beloved colleagues saw me loading up a stack of papers I'd collected to take home for weekend grading. "Leave 'em here," he said, and watched as I looked at him incredulously, clutching my papers tighter. "You're just going to take them for a ride in your car and bring them right back on Monday. Save yourself the agony and leave them on your desk. You can't spend your life grading papers." That moment of reckoning helped me realize that to be an effective teacher of writing, I had to abandon the idea that I had to grade everything. Once I realized that young writers need practice, practice, practice *but don't need me to assess every single thing they write, my writing instruction improved because I could focus on students. Finally.*

Now I spend the majority of my time with students in writing conferences: listening, posing questions, addressing small groups that have similar issues, reading and responding to drafts. All writing is for an authentic audience, and it's during conferences that I'm able to understand students' progress and understand their roadblocks as a fellow writer, not as a teacher giving a grade. By the time a piece of writing receives a "final for now" grade, both the writer and I are confident the work submitted is their best effort.

Once it's time for submission, and if the assignment needs to be graded (because not everything does), I then work with students to look closely at the mentor texts we've used throughout a writing study and at the work they've done to put together a student-created rubric. My writers determine what they think is integral to an effective piece and then take the lead to design a rubric they think captures the work they've completed. These discussions are always rich with students' considerations about craft, about attention to mentor texts, and, ultimately, about overall effectiveness of the piece. I've found that when students use these rubrics for their own self-reflection and I use these rubrics for my assessment, the correlation between product and grade is accurate. It's not unusual for students to want to revise their work after taking the lead in creating the rubric and reading their colleagues' drafts. Further, when I discuss the work with students, the rubric they've created provides a useful foundation for future writing and helps to facilitate productive conversations about assessment as we return to the rubric when appropriate, revising it as we go.

A RECENT (BRIEF) HISTORY OF THE ENGLISH TEACHER'S PAPER LOAD

History, we think, offers some sort of comfort and even perspective. The paper load is not a new problem, and the approaches to solutions are multiple. In past decades, public school systems across the United States have periodically acknowledged the extra workload of English teachers—and of social studies teachers too—and have made periodic efforts to reduce student numbers so that English teachers can more gracefully handle this kind of workload.

In Leila's state, Virginia Beach City Public Schools led the way for some years, assigning English teachers not the standard five but four classes a week so they could devote more time to their students' writing. In today's economy, however, reduced school funding is not friendly toward such accommodations (the Virginia Beach City Public Schools discontinued the English teacher reduced load for just such considerations), and today serious and fundable proposals for lessening English teachers' workloads rarely surface in any school board budget meeting. This is exacerbated in particular since recent reform efforts have defined all teachers as reading and writing teachers—without, of course, acknowledging the tremendous amount of extra labor this takes.

Looking back to much earlier in the history of teaching English, the paper load for English teachers was seriously discussed more than a century ago. In the first article of the first issue of *English Journal*, January 1912 (the publication just begun by the newly founded National Council of Teachers of English [NCTE]), a writing teacher raised this very subject. Edwin M. Hopkins taught at the University of Kansas, but his workload would not seem that out of line for many current middle school or high school teachers. Hopkins described the situation and decried the numbers:

> Not very many years ago, when effort was made to apply the principle that pupils should learn to write by writing, English composition . . . became ostensibly a laboratory subject[,] . . . a gratuitous increase in the labor of teachers who were already doing full duty. . . .
>
> [C]omposition teachers have from two and a half to three times as many pupils as they should. . . . [I]t is subjecting such teachers . . . to a physical and mental strain that is two and half times the ascertained limit of endurance[,] . . . two to five or six times as great as any similar duty of other teachers. Because of this, the average of the total labor devolving upon English composition teachers is apparently between 50 and 100 per cent more than the average total of that of any other class of teachers whatever. (2, 3)

Hopkins's heartfelt plea did not, in 1912, go unanswered, and indeed there was some change in English teachers' workloads across the nation. But today we can mostly agree that those advances are no longer in force, and while Hopkins predicted dire consequences—"Every year teachers resign, break down, perhaps become permanently invalided, having sacrificed ambition, health, and in not a few instances even life, in the struggle to do all the work expected of them" (1)—English teachers and their classes mostly rolled on. Today we might wonder whether the current teacher shortage and pattern of new teachers leaving the profession after the first three to five years is not, in English, related to being asked to do an impossible job and to resolve the contradictions solely through individual—even heroic—effort.

You, a veteran teacher, probably have some good ideas about how to handle these issues and would also welcome more. But if not, and if you are "solving" the time problem by assigning less writing than you know you really should, we would like you to consider some other avenues that can indeed address the serious dilemma of what a single teacher can do to respond to the frequent writing that we know students need to do.

Patricia A. Dunn, veteran teacher and author of several works on the teaching of writing, including *Talking, Sketching, Moving: Multiple Literacies in the Teaching of Writing*, suggests that when we respond to students' texts, we should keep in mind how much time *they* are willing to give *us*. Dunn is in our Teachers' Lounge now, ready to give us some advice about making the most of students' attention.

—— FROM THE TEACHERS' LOUNGE ——

Making the Most of the Few Minutes Students Will Give Your Response

Patricia A. Dunn
Stony Brook University, State University of New York

Students will spend no more than a few minutes reading a teacher's response to their writing, so it's important to work smart and plan for that limited time.

First, point out several things they're doing well. Those things depend, of course, on the genre they're writing (book review, how-to piece, blog, complaint letter, high-stakes test practice, travel narrative, etc.). Maybe they've nailed some technical conventions of a blog, or included vivid details in a travel narrative, or used effective parallel structure in their how-to piece. Maybe they've finally mastered the signposting conventions of the prompt-driven test essay. Or perhaps they're doing a good job varying sentence structure and length. Teachers should notice these things. Why? Because it builds confidence in writers who may badly need a reason to keep writing and revising.

Then, point out several things they should work on in a revision or next project. Again, genre dictates some features. Maybe in their travel narratives writers are raving about the beauty of a place but neglecting to tell us what they saw, heard, or smelled. In an argument, maybe they say parents should give teenagers more privacy, but they don't anticipate (and then handle) the reasons parents might want to know what their teens are up to. Maybe writers' word choice is too formal for a blog or too casual for a letter to the principal. Perhaps some well-placed statistics could support their argument, or a quick anecdote or snippet of dialogue could help keep readers' attention.

Once writers are happy with a developed draft, teachers can help diagnose patterns of error that need attention. For example, what are two errors this writer makes repeatedly? Point out a few cases where they occur, make sure writers know how to fix them, and then hold them responsible for eliminating those particular errors in the next draft or project. It helps to keep a record of which students need to work on what. Pick out a couple more error patterns in the next round, give a mini-lesson (or link to a site that does), and have students add these to the repertoire of errors they will no longer make. It's not possible to fix everything at once, but if edits are doable, writers are more likely to focus on and fix them. If there's pressure on you to mark every little thing you see, tell students (and parents) what you're doing and why.

Finally, experiment with different ways of responding: end comments, memos, marginal comments in Word or Google Docs, audio commentary, voice memos, screencasting, Skype-like video conferences, or one-on-one meetings if possible. Ask students what kinds of responses work best for them. Not every student will want or need the same kind of response or delivery method. Varying the tools you employ, the genres students write, and the different responses you give will make responding faster, more efficient, and more likely to help writers improve.

OTHER IDEAS FOR READING AND RESPONDING TO STUDENT WRITING
USE AN ARTIST'S PORTFOLIO

Although the national move to have students archive large chunks of their writing in a portfolio that could then be transmitted from teacher to teacher has somewhat abated, the idea of portfolios is still a viable one (see, for instance, Yancey, whose work is some of the best and very practical). Few teachers have the storage capacity—or the stamina—to safeguard or assess huge amounts of student work, but asking students to put in one folder, paper or electronic, representative samples of their work can be immeasurably helpful in dealing with the paper load. Students can put in their artist's portfolio daily writing, responses to essay tests, parts of a research paper, creative assignments, and other genre papers (e.g., argument, exposition) completed in the marking period or periods. Compiling this writing can encourage students immensely as they see the range and the amount of the work they have done. For teachers, it can also be a source of a quick overview of a student's writing history, and while every piece included in the portfolio may not have been read, responded to, and graded at the time, teachers can use the portfolio as the basis for an overall grade.

HAVE STUDENTS COLLECT REPRESENTATIVE PAPERS AND SELECT AND SUBMIT A LIMITED NUMBER FOR FINAL GRADING

In concert with this artist's portfolio, it's also possible for students to self-select a highly limited number of papers and, from that pool, designate one or two for final grading. Though some students may not like the limited nature of this pool of papers, if they have guidance in the selection and in the process, they can understand that this is a legitimate way to look at their writing production. It can, most obviously, also provide for the teacher a much more manageable number of papers to read and respond to.

RECONFIGURE THE RESEARCH PROJECT

For English teachers, the research project can be one of the most onerous of tasks. Students are asked to select a topic, research it, quote sources accurately, and prepare a bibliography. In our years of visiting schools, we have watched conscientious teachers struggle with topic selection, source search, and bibliographic format. Once submitted, the final product is often a trial to read and grade, and some teachers find themselves putting the work off for days, weeks, even months.

What can we do to address this? As veteran teachers, we have acquired some freedom and autonomy, and many of us are also aware that the "standard" literary research paper—often presented to our students as *You will need this in your English classes in college*—is not what it used to be. Few first-year college students or even sophomores write on the imagery in *The Scarlet Letter*, and even fewer analyze, as a research project, the plot points in *Huck Finn*. Why then do we put our students and ourselves through these kinds of contortions?

It's not that research is out of fashion; it's just that the kind of research we ask many of our students to do in our English classrooms is outdated. Asking students to pursue more relevant topics such as those used in real college classes and incorporating the multigenre approaches also often requested in college classes will more closely meet our students' needs if they indeed continue with their education.

Finally, grouping students in like-minded research groups can reduce the number of final papers to read and respond to, and setting up incremental point systems can ensure that when students submit a final paper, many of its components have already been read and evaluated.

INSTITUTE DAILY WRITING

If you think about any skill you have in your life or have attempted at some time in your life, you certainly recognize the crucial component of practice and frequency. Regardless of the task—brewing a perfect pot of tea, transplanting a rosebush, executing a layup shot that goes right into the basket, mastering a crossword puzzle, building a desk, winning some part of a video game—practice, if it doesn't make perfect, makes the task far easier and ultimately contributes to excellence. When our students are asked to write infrequently—and, at that, asked to write on relatively high-stakes assignments, even tests—they are often fearful and hesitant. They rarely have the fluency to complete this writing because, in truth, they don't write on a regular basis and thus don't write with any established confidence.

In a crowded curriculum, we can address this relatively easily and avoid disrupting lesson and unit plans by instituting short, daily writing. This writing begins every class, and starting with three to five minutes of writing gives students consistent, daily practice. It's not that difficult to do: if your students know that once the bell rings or the tone sounds they are supposed to get out a notebook or open their laptop to write, they are routinely learning to kick-start a writing response.

The topic of that writing can certainly change. It can be completely open—*Write for three to five minutes on anything*—or it can be targeted to a variety of topics. One target can be the day's work: *Select two adjectives that describe Hamlet and give one reason for each. Briefly outline one problem you are having with your research assignment. Write for five minutes on something interesting you learned about poetry in our class this week. Select one or two vocabulary words we have recently studied and explain why you would* ever *or* never *have occasion to use them.*

Another target can be something less focused: *Look at the quotation on the whiteboard and briefly discuss if you think it is true or not. Prom tickets are now on sale—what one or two changes would you like to see in this year's prom? This controversial film just hit the big screen—what do you think?*

At any rate, if the time to write is truly limited (and three to five minutes is not as short as you might imagine), most students will accomplish something in that period of time. Using a timer students can see can be a motivator, and for those who fret about the length of the assignment, those ticking seconds can be a comfort because students can monitor the time quickly passing. In addition, adding some sort of appropriate music to accompany the writing or even dimming the classroom overhead lights can help create and sustain a writing atmosphere. Now there are even websites designed to create adjustable coffeehouse sounds that function as white noise and help focus those of us who find such places conducive to work. (Check out Cafe Restaurant: https://mynoise.net/NoiseMachines/cafeRestaurant NoiseGenerator.php.)

USE DAILY WRITING TO SHAPE STUDENTS' MASTERY

Using daily writing can shape students' mastery, giving them fluency and practice as well as a sense of accomplishment regarding the sheer volume of writing they have been able to generate. And, as a teacher, you can create this situation by following some basic steps, the first of which involves the tone you set in your classroom. Making the three to five minutes work is a matter of repetition and reinforcement. As you start this practice, explaining to students what they are doing and why and then following through with virtually every class sets the consistent expectation that this is the first thing everyone does when class starts.

First, there needs to be **consistency**: the short writing is done virtually every class. Once students know that this is the start of their class, they will follow through with the procedure. This, of course, doesn't mean that every class period every student will write great prose or even a lot of it, but the setting and the opportunity are established.

You should establish a writing **community** in which you participate: you as the teacher should stop what you are doing and write with your students. Students will see you with your notebook or laptop and not doing other (yes, important, but also distracting) classroom tasks, and they will soon understand that this writing stuff is for everyone, not just them. Writing *with* students is one of the most powerful things you can do. And when you ask your students to share their writing, you share yours too sometimes. As a veteran teacher, your confident vulnerability can be beyond powerful, and we know you and your ego are up to it!

RESPOND TO DAILY WRITING

Does daily writing always need a response? No. But occasional responses can take many forms: Students can swap papers and talk about them for a minute or two, or write a comment. Students can be selected (randomly or on some regular volunteer basis) to read their writing out loud and get a reaction from the class. You can collect just a few and respond briefly to them. Other times, the writing can remain in a notebook of other writing you may eventually read. And, on days that you do collect this writing, you can use it toward participation credit and even use it to take attendance.

But how does a teacher respond to the writing that students generate in a significant yet sustainable manner?

As an initial step, decide whether you wish to look at your students' daily writing on a one-, two-, or three-week basis. At the very beginning, we recommend doing this **every week** because what you "give back" to students will be reinforcing. After that, however, you can certainly respond to the daily writing—looking at their paper notebooks or the electronic writing files—every **two to three weeks**. We recommend the following as options, any of which we believe may well fit your classroom goals and your students.

> ▶ **Skim all weekly entries and mark each page; make a global response at the end.** If you put a mark on each page (a check, for example) either by hand or electronically, depending on how the weekly writing is submitted, students will be assured that you have viewed each page (and you will also be sure you haven't missed any pages). You can also, if this suits you, write a general response: *thanks for sharing; this shows thought; keep up the good work*, etc. As an addition, you can mark with a ★ any section of the writing to note *I like this; I agree*. While these generic responses aren't wholly satisfying because they don't address specifics, they do the job of acknowl-

edging your students' writing. And, since you will have occasionally incorporated responses to these writings on the days they were written, you'll know that students did get more response earlier than you're giving this time.

▸ **Count all weekly pages, skim and check; make general response.** Adding to the above practice, you can reinforce the writing by indicating the number of pages your students have generated (for example, 5/5 for a week; 4/10 for two weeks, depending on the completed entries), and even tie that to a grade. If students have three to five minutes every class to write and, when you look at their work, can show you only a few completed pages, then they need to know they aren't making the best use of their time. Doing the classic freewriting technique ("I have no ideas but I will keep the keyboard or my hand moving by writing 'I have no ideas I have no ideas' until the ideas come . . .") may also be important to introduce there. (And by the way, if you aren't familiar with freewriting, you might check out Peter Elbow's massively influential work *Writing with Power*.) Nevertheless, your generic response is similar to that listed in the previous bullet (though it could well be tied to the numbers: *Great effort here; Keep up the good work*) as well as the marking or starring of a short section.

▸ **Select one entry from the week or weeks; read and respond.** As students become more adept at daily writing, it is quite possible for you to randomly select a single entry for the week or weeks, actually read it word for word (not skim), and respond to it. This can be reinforcing for students who wish more than the general comment from you, and it can, mixed with the other practices outlined here, give you real insight into your students' use of and response to daily writing. It's especially important with this kind of impromptu, zero-draft writing (writing that hasn't yet even been formed into a coherent first draft) for you to focus on praise and conversational response, not negative criticism.

▸ **Have students select one entry from the week or weeks; read and respond.** Giving students control of the practice, outlined above, and letting *them* select the one entry they wish you to respond to can reinforce student control and autonomy. It can give you a sense of what students value in this daily writing or what, at least at this point, they are comfortable or interested in having you read. It also confines your reading and response time to a single entry.

WORKING WITH MORE EXTENSIVE WRITING

Beyond the daily writing, however, are the frequent situations when you and your students embark on a more extensive writing task, one that might involve a series of drafts of arguments, stories, expositions, and research that could include primary and secondary sources. Many of the assignments suggested in the previous chapter focus on authentic writing (for real audiences), and those assignments require and deserve greater depth of response.

If you are like most teachers, you scaffold longer assignments and provide multiple segments that have deadlines and point components. While some adept students can work on a long assignment without such scaffolding, experience teaches us that most students require checkpoints—and grade-based encouragement—along the way. And even advanced students will require more scaffolding for projects that are more sophisticated and complex than they've dealt with previously.

Once students have preliminary drafts, however, the issue for you again is how to respond. While you will need to be sure that all students have completed this part of the assignment, in-depth response can be accomplished in small groups.

ATTITUDES AND METHODS FOR SUSTAINABLE RESPONSE

How have veteran teachers who engage their students in continuous writing, have satisfying professional worlds, and enjoy happy, balanced personal lives found the magic bullet? Do they know a secret that others don't that gives them more hours in the day? Setting aside possible deals with devils and ancient pedagogical relics with mystical powers (okay, we're kidding), probably not. Instead, it's likely these teachers have developed attitudes and methods of response that enable and empower their students and don't depend entirely on one teacher's time.

Here are nine attitudes and principles that help teachers develop sustainable response practices:

- Writing is valuable in itself, and not every piece of writing you assign students needs response. Sometimes just having written is its own reward. One of NCTE's helpful statements, *Professional Knowledge for the Teaching of Writing,* reminds us: "People learn to write by writing."

- Another NCTE principle in the same document states, "Writing is a process and a tool for thinking." Teachers can incorporate writing that will receive oral feedback in conversation, rather than a written response.

- Teachers' responses are not of unlimited value. Yes, our perspectives and judgments are useful, especially if we are going to be the sole arbiter of grades, but we have only our own experience to work with. Early career teachers can perhaps be forgiven for seeing themselves at the center of their students' learning. Veteran teachers, however, accept that students will learn from other people, other resources, and other experiences—often even more than they will from us. Harnessing those learning experiences with others for ELA purposes will assist teachers in saving their own time.

- Helping students experience multiple perspectives on their writing is far better for helping them develop portable writing skills than will many, many responses from a single teacher.

- When we respond to students' writing, we should do so with specific purposes in mind and narrow our responses to those purposes. One response should not try to address all aspects of a piece of writing. Often a light touch is better than an extensive—and even intense—response.

- Different stages of writing processes require different forms of response. Brainstorming and early drafts require encouragement to find new ideas and options for expansion. Drafting and revising require examination and reexamination of what students may have already decided is good enough. Late stage drafts require close attention to details and a disciplined attitude toward correctness.

▸ Teachers are *not* copyeditors. Copyediting is actually rigorous professional work that requires a high level of expertise that the great majority of teachers do not have. As former *English Journal* editors, we can attest to the fact that most English teachers don't copyedit effectively. It's okay. That's why copyediting is a profession! In fact, Ken negotiated for a professional copy editor for *EJ* before he accepted the position as editor. "I get way too caught up in the ideas in a manuscript to be effective at ensuring all the wording and conventions are correct and as clear as possible," says Ken. We are—or at least Ken is—quite sure that Theresa Kay, *EJ*'s copy editor for more than fifteen years now, would agree that Ken needed help. (We emailed Theresa, and she did, with quite a disturbing level of emphasis, agree. She then suggested our email could use a copyedit.)

▸ Consider the value of collaborative writing. If three to five students produce a single draft, that generates far fewer drafts than if each student writes his or her own. NCTE's *Professional Knowledge for the Teaching of Writing* notes that "a good deal of workplace writing and other writing occurs in collaborative situations."

▸ Students benefit from reflecting on their own writing and from responding to the writing of other students. These experiences reinforce several important "habits of mind" that effective writers must develop: openness, engagement, creativity, flexibility, and metacognition. These habits of mind and others may be found in the *Framework for Success in Postsecondary Writing*, a collaborative report written by the Council of Writing Program Administrators, NCTE, and the National Writing Project.

CONCLUSION: SUSTAINING THE RESPONDER

Frequent writing is essential to solid English instruction, but without techniques in place, even committed veteran teachers can be utterly overwhelmed by the tsunami of work that responding to any kind of student writing assignment can generate. As a primary responder, you need to take care of yourself too so that you always have the energy, attitude, and patience that effective response to student writing requires. Using some of the techniques outlined in this chapter for significant yet sustainable practices can help you, as a smart veteran with limited time, to be both responsible to your students and respectful of that one person you may often tend to forget—yourself.

Making Audience Matter: Counting Real-World Feedback

It's all well and good to talk to students about the importance of audience and real-world aspects of writing. Unless we actually work to ensure that real-world feedback from outside audiences is factored into the grades students receive on their writing, that's all it is, just so much talk.

If we're going to engage students in authentic writing, we have to make the feedback from real audiences count. And that kind of counting includes the final grade.

Let's be clear at the outset: we know this isn't the easiest way to teach and assess writing. Getting outside feedback on students' writing requires innovation, risk-taking, and a willingness to ask others for help. Thus the old adage of shutting the classroom door and doing your own thing won't entirely work if you're going to teach writing authentically and open that writing to outside audiences. To do this, you will have to open your door to select others and ask them to contribute to your students' development. And you have to be willing to take the risks associated with encouraging your students to write for outside audiences.

Once again, this is the kind of step we know that you, as a veteran teacher, are not only prepared to take but also can take with confidence. In this chapter, we help to show you how.

In the following pages, we explore ways to bring outside audiences to your students. Some of these techniques require adaptation for different grade levels, but they are all available to teachers at any level of writing instruction. So we ask you to approach this chapter with an open mind and a sense of play, and you'll find lots of ideas for bringing authentic audiences to your students' writing assignments. It's just another of the many ways you can take advantage of your strength and expertise as a veteran teacher.

First, let's look at a highly accomplished veteran teacher to see what he does in his classroom.

INVITING THE AUDIENCE INTO THE CLASSROOM

Well-known English teacher Jim Burke often invites members of his local California business community into his high school classes to interact with students on writing assignments that reflect the kind of writing that happens in the working world. In a particularly instructive *English Journal* article, "Connecting the Classroom, Community, and Curriculum," Burke details a unit he developed for his students on résumé writing. The unit culminated in real feedback from an audience of active business professionals who read the students' résumés and interviewed the students for a job. We highlight some of Burke's major ideas here (but his article is still a must-read).

Burke's reasoning for implementing a résumé unit with his high school seniors was primarily to give them a "reality check" about what the real working world requires from its employees: level of formal education, kinds of skills, specific ways of presenting oneself professionally, and so on. Within this framework, he developed a unit to assist students in both understanding the purposes of a résumé and in writing their own. Burke provided a mentor text and helped the students to understand which of their skills and experiences would be beneficial to list on their résumés.

This accounting of their experiences proved especially instructive for some students; for example, one student who was averaging a D in the class had far more extensive and interesting work and volunteer experience (at his church) than did an A student who generally went right home after school and prioritized homework and study. Part of the cleverness of Burke's approach is that while learning to write a rigid, somewhat academic genre (in this case, a résumé), students simultaneously learned more about the real-world value of extra-academic experience—and about themselves. This is one way of allowing an authentic genre to open up students' thinking.

So far, this may seem like a fairly ordinary résumé-writing unit; but, rather than allow the discussion to remain academic, Burke called in the help of a local business professional, Mike Heffernan, president of the local Rotary Club. Together, Burke and Heffernan hatched a plan to ask more Rotary members to come to Burke's class and conduct practice interviews with students, who would be applying for an imagined position as an assistant for a bail bonds company. They also developed together some common interview questions so they could establish "a sort of common baseline for comparison" (21).

In preparation for the day of interviewing, Burke created what he calls "interim lessons" on design (constructing a résumé), social media, and "reality" (21–23). Students balked at how little time real employers actually take to read applicants' résumés and that employers almost always do internet searches of applicants' names to see if any controversial information pops up, especially on social media.

The day of interviews arrived, and eight volunteer Rotarians interviewed all thirty-five of Burke's students in a single period (about five minutes per student). If the unit had stopped there, the results would have been completely satisfactory, but the next step is what makes this experience truly valuable: the business leaders provided real feedback to the class (emailed that night from Heffernan to Burke) so that students would learn how their work went over with a real audience, and Burke could factor this feedback into the students' grades. In fact, Burke and Heffernan decided that having Heffernan come back to deliver the feedback in person would have even more impact (24). Heffernan spent an entire period with the students giving feedback such as the following:

- ▸ "Generally, the students were prepared, except for 2 who did not know the job responsibilities. Those 2 did a good job for the rest of the interview but they lost out in terms of **'first impression'**—and it's rare that you can ever totally recover."

- ▸ "Each of them **looked me in the eye** on more than one occasion. Good!"

- ▸ "I wish they had **used my name** at least once. I tried to use their name several times, hoping that would encourage them to use my name. Using the interviewer's name is important—you paid attention; it's respectful." (24)

Jim also received feedback from Beth Pascal, his high school's school-to-work coordinator, who suggested adding an individual feedback sheet (so each student would see specific information about his or her performance) and graphing some of the feedback (so students could visualize the aggregated data) (26).

One of Burke's student's comments in his reflection on the class unit sum up best, for Burke, what he thought this unit's value was:

> I feel that this will help me greatly down the road in gaining valuable experience needed. I also now have a better understanding of what employers look for in a résumé and an interview.
>
> I really appreciated Mrs. [Beth] Pascal coming in and demonstrating what not to do in front of an adult when you are interviewing or applying for a job. I also appreciated the critique I received from the Rotary person [Heffernan] about my job interview and look to carry what I learned into the real world. (Burke, "Connecting" 27)

These kinds of authentic lessons are particularly important for students to experience, as Burke puts it, "before graduating into their larger lives in the community where they must find their place and, with it, a sense of purpose and a feeling of pride" (27).

We also find Burke's article doubly inspiring because of what it is not. This is not an article about a successful unit a veteran teacher has honed over many years. Rather, it's an account of a teacher's first attempt at doing something new and risky. Burke ends his discussion with some thoughts about the unit:

> Perhaps the most important lesson of this unit for me—remember, you are reading about the first time I did any of this—is that it's OK to jump first and figure it out later so long as you are guided by the right principles and get good people to help you along the way. I did not reject or ignore any element of the English curriculum, nor was I reckless; I simply accomplished more with the material than I was otherwise expected to do. Another crucial decision: I sought out and used those resources—within school and the larger community—that could help me

III

achieve these more ambitious ends. To that end, Beth Pascal and Mike Heffernan (and those Rotarians he recruited) were instrumental. ("Connecting" 27)

If Jim Burke, a veritable giant in our field, can publicly acknowledge the anxieties that come with taking risks in the curriculum and his need to ask for help from others, then surely the rest of us should feel okay about taking the risks that authentic writing instruction and authentic feedback require. Like you, we also have those feelings of vulnerability as we strike out for new curricular territory and reach out to initiate new relationships with partners for our students' benefit.

As with Burke's résumé writing unit, sometimes a whole school can engage together in an assignment that brings the community into the process of educating the area's young people. For example, Christopher Scanlon, a teacher in Florida, works in a school that has created a capstone project for all seniors that requires the students to make presentations to a panel of outside judges and then receive specific feedback from those judges, whose real-world responses are then calculated in the students' grades. Stopping by our Teachers' Lounge, Scanlon is able to take a quick a break from his senior class to tell us what he likes about this assignment.

─── FROM THE TEACHERS' LOUNGE ───

Students Present to Outside Judges

Christopher Scanlon
Belleview High School, Belleview, Florida

I'm fortunate to work in a high school that goes to great lengths to provide a rigorous education for all its students, at every level. To that end, it is a graduation requirement for each senior to complete a capstone project. The student must research a possible career choice, and then do or create something that will provide them with a learning stretch. Many

of them intern or shadow someone in their chosen field. Others take the hands-on approach, rebuilding a truck engine or building a working model of a hydroelectric generator, for instance. A research paper detailing their learning stretch is the first project element that is assessed.

The final part of the project, and the one that produces the most anxiety, is a presentation of students' learning. This happens over the course of two evenings, when the students present to a panel made up of people from the community, including businesspeople, district administrators, local politicians, practitioners in the chosen field, and, yes, some teachers. The panel will not only hear the presentations, but also ask probing questions to determine the breadth of the students' knowledge.

What I like most about this is the confidence the students earn. I provide my students with a rigorous experience, but I'm biased—I like them and want them to succeed. They know my quirks and hot buttons and can play to my preferences. Not here. On this night, the students must walk into an unknown situation, armed only with the learning they have procured for themselves. They have to read the room to make last-minute adjustments, then step into the abyss. They have to face this alone. The parallels to a job interview are not lost on anyone. If they do well (and most do), they can be reasonably certain they have developed transferable skills that can be mapped onto real-world situations outside of a school.

Some do poorly. They were counting on their charisma to make up for an utter lack of preparation. They tried to wing something they most definitely should not have tried to wing. This too is a lesson, if they are wise enough to learn it.

When it's over, the students receive an average of the judges' three scores as the presentation grade. Even better, the judges' actual rubrics are available to the students after the grades are complete. [See Belleview High School's rubric template below.[2]] A surprising number of students

request the rubrics. I take this as evidence that, despite their initial objec-
tions to the project, most students see the value in an authentic assess-
ment of their work by an objective outside audience.

Belleview High School (Florida) Senior Capstone Presentation Rubric

Student Name:	Judge Name:
Please evaluate the student presentation on a scale of 1–100. **100 – Superior; 90 – Excellent; 80 – Good; 70 – Average; 60 – Fair; 30–50 – Poor; 0–20 – Not Evident** Please look for these characteristics:	
Content: Effective introduction Speech controlled by a clearly stated purpose Logical organization Main Idea supported by accurate and effective details Conclusion	**30 Points Possible:** ____
Product: Involves a learning stretch Demonstrates a level of difficulty that requires a sustained effort	**30 Points Possible:** ____
Delivery: Appropriate voice, volume, speed Eye contact with audience Appropriate word choice Evidence of practice beyond reading of notes Effective gestures Attitude: energy, enthusiasm, and personalization Composure	**20 Points Possible:** ____
Impromptu Skills: Direct, clear answers Complete thoughts Elaborated answers Appropriate language	**10 points possible:** ____
Dress/Appearance: Professional appearance	**10 points possible:** ____
Final Grade	**Total out of 100 Points:** ____
Judge's Comments:	

INCORPORATING REAL-WORLD FEEDBACK INTO CLASS ASSIGNMENTS

In his Methods of Teaching English classes at Stony Brook University, Ken has employed several forms of authentic writing that use peer response groups and real outside feedback as part of the grade. One project required the students to prepare an essay to submit to the "Teacher to Teacher" feature in *English Journal*. This feature asked a question related to a specific issue's theme, and *EJ* would publish the best of the approximately 350-word submissions received from all over the country. Some of the questions included:

- What is something you've done as a teacher that took guts? (July 2013 issue)

- What literature fosters the examination of bullying behaviors? (July 2012 issue)

- What literature related to the environment and nature do you enjoy teaching? (January 2011 issue)

- What kinds of collaboration do you engage in for the benefit of your students? (May 2010 issue)

The students composed their responses to the question, and then they worked them through a pretty rigorous peer response session. In small groups, the students read and responded to the drafts of another group; then the group of writers and the group of responders met to discuss the feedback. Because the essays were so short (350 words), there was lots of time for deep response.

Figure 7.1 is the peer feedback sheet Ken created that included the grade additions. Although this feedback sheet was for college-level students, it was intended to model a peer feedback sheet that would be more appropriate for secondary and middle school writers, since these college students were studying to become teachers at these grade levels. Note in particular that the number lines and the breakdown of questions would ordinarily be less explicit in college-level peer feedback sheets.

Writing for a Real Audience PEER RESPONSE SHEET
"Teacher to Teacher" Essays Written for *English Journal* and a Panel of Area English Teachers
EGL 441/CEE 588, K. Lindblom

Respondents should base all their answers upon their knowledge of the "Teacher to Teacher" column and their knowledge of the assignment. Remember that in addition to the *English Journal* audience, the panel of area English teachers is also an important audience for this essay.

These responses will be collected with the final drafts; reviewers whose comments substantially contribute to any of the top three essays will be acknowledged in print on the English Teacher Education Program Blackboard Site and a 1/3 letter grade will be added to their assignment grade (e.g., B will become a B+, C+ will become a B-, etc.).

Peer Respondent's Name: ______________________________

Writer's Name: ______________________________

For the **Respondent** to Answer:

1. How effectively does the author give the information the selected question asks for?

This paper does not really answer the question.	←1—2—3—4—5—6—7—8—9—10→	This paper gives precisely the kind of information the question is asking for.

2. What information is missing from the essay and/or what information presently in the essay is not relevant to the question?

3. How effectively do the author's words create an appropriate voice and character for English teachers who are readers of *English Journal*?

This essay does not sound appropriately authoritative.	←1—2—3—4—5—6—7—8—9—10→	This essay reads as if it were written by an expert who writes for *EJ* regularly.

4. How should the author consider revising to create a better impression on readers?

5. How effectively does the author's tone, register, and writing style work in the essay?

This paper is inappropriately informal or formal, sarcastic, monotonous, or otherwise ineffective in style.	←1—2—3—4—5—6—7—8—9—10→	The level of prose used, the wit or cleverness of the writing, the level of seriousness, and other related matters are brilliantly effective.

FIGURE 7.1. Ken's peer response sheet for writing for a real audience.

FIGURE 7.1. Continued.

6. How should the author consider revising to better take advantage of the opportunities tone, register, and writing style provide a writer in this rhetorical situation?

7. How original and creative is the author's idea or the way the author composed the essay?

This essay is completely unsurprising and does not show any creative flair.

←1—2—3—4—5—6—7—8—9—10→

The idea expressed is completely new and is described very creatively.

8. What could the author do to make the idea more original and/or make the writing more imaginative?

9. How effectively does this paper attend to the submission guidelines and other conventions (format, surface errors, font, etc.) this audience will expect the paper to adhere to?

This paper seems completely out of synch with what the audience is likely to expect.

←1—2—3—4—5—6—7—8—9—10→

This paper very effectively follows and/or very effectively breaks the rules expected by this audience.

10. What should the author consider adding, deleting, or revising to more effectively fit the submission guidelines and other rules the audience will expect the essay to follow?

For the **Writer** to Answer:
Given the above respondent's advice, what specific revisions will you strongly consider making to your paper?

Following the peer response workshops, Ken could simply have required students to write and submit essays for this feature, but he knew they wouldn't receive much (if any) feedback from the *EJ* editor. And even if they did receive feedback, it wouldn't be truly outside response since their teacher was also, coincidentally, editor of *EJ* at the time. (*Awkward!*) So instead, Ken arranged for a panel of three veteran English teachers to read the entire set of class responses. The members of the panel were each asked to read all the short essays, pick their three favorites, and explain what they liked about them.

Here's some of the feedback received for students' "Teacher to Teacher" essays about bullying behaviors. The reviewer (one of three) is Emily Puccio, a local English educator; the numbers correspond to the essays she selected, as the student authors' names were not revealed:

1. This was my favorite "Teacher to Teacher" essay. I loved the authenticity of the author's perspective, and the examples that the author selected to emphasize the position were constructive for the reader and thought-provoking. The writing itself was strongly articulated and professional. The author did not "waste" any words, rather s/he chose to dive right into the topic and present the case (as opposed to other essays, that seemed to have a protracted introduction where none was necessary).

12. The strength of this essay is that it answered the question very directly. The response was broad enough to be applicable in all situations, yet specific enough to provide something tangible for a teacher to take back to the classroom. Further, it did not simply suggest that—by following the example one situation provides—the question of knowing students can always be answered. The response was relatable to me as a teacher, I agree with the position the writer takes, and I think that this position is something that more teachers need to internalize in their teaching. It reminds me of something a mentor said that sticks with me every day: "Remember, before they're your students, they're children."

8. This writer didn't only discuss ways to use literature to address the bullying issue, s/he codified why we can use literature successfully in the essay title with the words inspiring empathy. That we can inspire empathy is what makes the potential of the English classroom so powerful, and this is what our purpose is in using issue-based texts in our classrooms. So often, teachers focus on the "what" they're doing but not as much on the "why" (other than, because we need them to know that bullying is wrong). But move beyond "bullying is wrong." Let's inspire empathy. Well said. I also loved the approach that the writer suggested to inspire empathy (cutting the entries about bullying into anonymous texts for response).

Ken shared this feedback with the entire class, and, as previously announced to the class, the panelists' top three selections automatically got an A for the assignment and were announced and published on the Stony Brook University English Teacher Education Program's website. Ken and his class talked openly about his and their judgments of the works selected and others, and many interesting conversations arose about writing for real audiences versus writing for a teacher. This assignment was also fun because the students enjoyed writing for what they knew would be a real audience, and they especially appreciated that what they were writing about was something they were deeply interested in.

While this assignment was done in a college class, it need not be confined to that level. Middle and secondary school classes, which don't often consist of students who are all so invested in the same subject, need to allow students to choose from more forums to suit their interests. (As *EJ* editor, Ken also instituted a feature for middle and secondary students titled "Student Voices" to create exactly this kind of space.) But the magic really came from the fact that Ken was not entirely in control of the feedback and the grades. As a result, when the students met in peer response groups, their advice was every bit as helpful as Ken's, if not more so.

Ken used this assignment for several years, until a few veteran teachers he asked balked at the prospect of "grading his papers for him." That is, they seemed to resent the fact that they were doing Ken's work. Ken always offered to respond to those teachers' assignments in kind, but the teachers never took him up on his offer. So eventually he began to have two methods classes respond to each other's "Teacher to Teacher" essays in the same way the teachers had previously. It was not quite as effective, but the students found the opportunity to judge others' work to be an opportunity rather than a burden. Clearly, one of the important hurdles to be tackled in education is breaking down barriers between teachers (especially the barriers created by their workload) so more productive collaborations can occur.

High school English teacher and past president of the Michigan Council of Teachers of English Andy Schoenborn also encourages his students to write for real audiences through several venues. He's designed a clever set of classroom assignments that engage students in a process that models genuine, peer-reviewed publication. He's stopped by our Teachers' Lounge to tell us more about it.

FROM THE TEACHERS' LOUNGE

The Value of Authentic Feedback

Andy Schoenborn
Mt. Pleasant High School, Mt. Pleasant, Michigan

Ask any writer and they will tell you that when you write for real audiences, the writing game changes. The tendency is to pull back a bit to protect ourselves from the vulnerability writers feel. Knowing your audience is interested and intelligent builds a tension that is equally daunting and exhilarating.

This is normal. It is all part of an authentic writing process.

I remember the first time I told students to publish their work on YouTube. The room went silent. A student raised her hand and said, "But, Mr. Schoenborn, if we put our videos on YouTube that means we actually have to try."

Bingo.

Yes, if we take the risk to put ourselves in a public forum and "go for the rejection letter," it means we actually have to try.

Since then I seek opportunities for students to share, receive, and respond to feedback beyond the classroom. I often plan units with authentic audiences in mind. If students are reading young adult novels, for instance, I ask them to craft and share a guest blog post with me as a reviewer. During my review, I ask them to share a specific focus they would like me to address; I share my reviewer expectations; give reviewer comments; and ask that they respond to my comments—all on a feedback sheet that can be seen using the QR code included here.

The process is the same as the process I have experienced as a writer.

After receiving and responding to my comments, students submit their posts to the Nerdy Book Club, *where they may be published as a guest blogger. We celebrate those who get published and experience the thrill together.*

Receiving feedback from authentic audiences adds value to any assignment, but, like any writing endeavor, waiting for authentic responses requires patience. When the responses come in, students feel the value of their work and are intrinsically motivated to continue the conversation.

Creating online spaces such as Live Write (livewrite.edublogs.org), where students showcase their work, increases the amount of feedback students receive. Coupled with a robust personal learning network on Twitter, as well as drawing on followers of @NCTE, @ILA, and @writing project, the feedback loop speeds up. When they look at the social media analytics of their posts, students feel validated and valued. I have learned that simply putting videos on YouTube is not enough. To see themselves as writers, students need to enter the game—that is, get real feedback from real audiences. When students feel the impact their voice has on their audience, their confidence soars and the writing game takes on new meaning.

ACKNOWLEDGING THE WORK OF PEER RESPONSE

As we discuss in a previous chapter, peer response requires significant work from both students and teachers, and it is only successful if everyone takes their efforts seriously. In the real world, writers often assist one another with peer feedback; in fact, academic knowledge is generally created in an anonymous peer review system. Savvy readers may have realized that in the unit discussed above, Ken's students in peer response groups would actually be competing with each other to be in the top three spots. Why would students give helpful feedback to writers with whom they are competing when they could instead sabotage their peers' efforts? Ken didn't actually believe his students would sabotage each other, but for the sake of a legitimate, real-world assignment, it was an important question to ponder. To address this to at least some degree, Ken devised a grading system that would reward peers for their substantial, helpful feedback: the top three essays would receive As, and the peers who gave them substantial feedback would receive an addition of one-third of a letter grade to their own essay score.

This assignment is fairly complex and takes time to plan; however, the students are motivated to succeed more than on other assignments because it is authentic. Students are writing for a real audience, they are receiving feedback from a real audience, and they are being judged and credited based on that feedback from that real audience. The authentic nature of the assignment also changes the relationship between the teacher and the students. No longer the sole judge and jury for the students' writing, the teacher can now be more of a guide, someone to run ideas by and to get advice from. And as the teacher, Ken was as interested to see the judge's feedback as the students were.

Ken's colleague Nicole Galante teaches the Advanced Methods of Teaching English course at Stony Brook University. Nicole and Ken collaborated on another authentic assessment a few years later in which the students in the advanced class worked in groups to design brochures and then later infographics about their choice of important concepts taught in the first methods class. As a result, after the first couple of weeks of class, the introductory students received helpful information about specific, foundational concepts—such as differentiated instruction, Vygotsky's zone of proximal development, reading fluency, and others—from their more advanced peers. And then the introductory students filled out a Google Form about the brochures or infographics that allowed the advanced methods students to see how helpful the introductory students found their texts. The advanced methods students also used the assignment as a way to better understand how authentic assignments can be used in their future classes. In addition, Nicole used the results of her advanced students' brochures or infographics to assess how well the students understood the concepts Ken had taught them the previous semester, enabling her to customize her instruction.

STANDARDIZED EXAM WRITING

Authentic assignments are fine, but practical veteran teachers may also ask about standardized exam writing. How do we help students pass—or excel in—writing exams? Our answer is immediate: even as artificial a rhetorical situation as an essay on a standardized exam can be, treating an exam as an authentic situation can help students succeed on those exams. Let's explore.

Many features of standardized test writing make it apparently inauthentic: strict time limits, contrived topics, inability to incorporate feedback and revision, and an overemphasis on argument writing. Still, we think standardized writing tests are, to some degree at least, legitimate examples of authentic writing; after all, the writing has a real purpose (a high score), a real context (state test writing genre), and is written for a real audience (state test graders). The problem is this type of writing is rare in the world outside of school, and yet it is too often taught as the only "correct" writing because of the high stakes attached to standardized exams. Teaching even this form of writing as an authentic assignment has benefits for students. And it can help students in those experiences outside school when they may need to address an on-demand writing situation, such as filling out an accident report at work, writing up testimony in a legal dispute, or leaving a quick note for someone.

Try some some of these activities, adapted from an article Ken wrote for NCTE's *English Leadership Quarterly* ("Treating" 10–11):

> ▸ Invite a "state writing examiner" (really, just another teacher or school administrator dressed as an "examiner") to your classroom and have students interview him or her about what she or he looks for in standardized exam writing and why. (With tongue firmly in cheek, we imagine someone intimidating like J. K. Rowling's Dolores Umbridge from *Harry Potter and the Order of the Phoenix.*) This can be done seriously, or the students can be in on the play aspects of this imaginative interview situation. When the interview is over, have students write it up and use it as a study guide for test writing.

> ▸ Think about the real rhetorical situation of state test writing: the writing prompt doesn't give the real rhetorical situation; it gives a fake one. The authentic prompt is: "What would a state writing examiner expect to read in an essay written to address the following prompt . . . ?" Recasting a standardized exam writing prompt this way can help students understand that they really are writing for a specific— and unusually powerful—audience of real people. We also find that especially savvy students appreciate this more directly honest approach to standardized exams.

> ▸ Encourage students to do some research on what really works in standardized exam writing, and help them publish guides or tip sheets for other students to succeed on them. This research and writing will not only engage students in the study of what works on exams, but it will also engage them in authentic writing at the same time. Students writing to other students for real purposes can be a mainstay of authentic writing.

WHEN A REAL AUDIENCE ISN'T AVAILABLE:
INCORPORATING PSEUDO-AUTHENTIC FEEDBACK

As much as we advocate for and value truly authentic writing assignments, we also know that they are not always feasible. Sometimes it's enough to add authentic elements to an assignment that will not genuinely engage a real outside audience. As we describe in Chapter 3, we call these kinds of assignments "pseudo-authentic." We don't intend *pseudo* as a negative term, but we want to acknowledge that assignments that have imagined audiences are not truly authentic, and thus they are less valuable than fully authentic assignments.

Despite this limitation, pseudo-authentic assignments can be excellent and are well worth including in classes focused on writing. Such assignments can have some of the same impact as authentic assignments, and they can energize students and engage teachers' creativity without generating a huge amount of outside work. Pseudo-authentic assignments are also a great first step toward creating a truly authentic assignment.

Consider starting with an assignment that adds some elements of authenticity this year, and then next year try expanding the assignment further, including a real audience. For example, a few years ago Ken taught a nonfiction course that attracted a large number of non-English majors. One of the themes of the course was happiness theory, and Ken used that theme to engage students in a wide study of different genres used in the world to communicate information, including academic articles, infographics, TED Talks and similar video presentations, tweets, opinion pieces, advertisements, and more. He wanted to create an assignment that would require students not only to use what they learned about happiness theory in the class, but also (and more important) to explore the rhetorical impact of the various nonfiction genres they had studied. His final project for that unit was a pseudo-authentic assignment (see Figure 7.2). The assignment memo is from an imagined company, Happiness, Inc., which spreads happiness and at which the students supposedly work as Happiness Recruiters. They must write a report to assist the company in hiring an effective Happiness Communicator. To do a good job with their report, the students will have to explain what effective rhetorical strategies are and what they look like in the kinds of genres the Happiness Communicator will be expected to be an expert in. So the report really requires the students to discuss more about rhetoric and nonfiction than about happiness. A separate sheet explains to the students some of the more specific expectations of their report:

> Midterm Paper Directions: Complete the report that is described in the scenario on the next page. The scenario is an imagined rhetorical situation, but you should take it seriously as an authentic situation. To complete the assignment, you must refer with *great depth* to 2–3 primary texts from our class about happiness: one must be a traditional text (article, book chapter, study), and one must be an infographic. As you discuss these primary texts, you should make substantial reference to the secondary texts we have read (the texts about rhetoric, about logic, and about infographics). You may refer to texts we have not read in class, but it is not required. Your report should be 6–10 pages long (1500–2500 words), not including title page, works cited page, or your cover memo on letterhead. (Yes, you should include a cover memo on letterhead.) In your report, please use in-text MLA Documentation for your sources.

This assignment essentially asks the students to address two rhetorical situations: (1) they are writing a report to an imagined company to assist them in hiring a "Happiness Communicator," and (2) they are writing a paper to a teacher that will demonstrate their expertise in the rhetoric of nonfiction.

A rubric helped the students understand the specific requirements by which their report would be graded, and also helped to emphasize the audience-based logic of the assignment (see Figure 7.3). Ken filled in the first set of criteria himself (which helps to define some of the more sophisticated concepts), and then had the students fill in the rest of the rubric in small groups. In this manner, the rubric serves as a scaffold for the students' thinking through the rhetorical situations embedded in the assignment.

Happiness, Inc.

Welcome to Happiness!

To: EGL 364 Student
From: I. Ken Employu, CEO, Happiness, Inc.
Re: Your Assistance with Our Efforts to Recruit an Effective "Happiness Communicator"
Date: February 20, 2018

Congratulations! You have been hired as Assistant Recruiter for our company, Happiness, Inc. As you know, our company mission is *to spread as effectively and in as many ways as possible good, quality information about how people can truly become happy*. We have hired you because you have shown a sincere interest in happiness, and we know you bring with you a wealth of knowledge about rhetoric, which we hope will allow you to assist us in our efforts to hire an excellent Happiness Communicator (HC). I write below with your first assignment with our new, growing company. If you do well on this assignment, you will receive a bonus, and you may even be considered for the position of senior recruiter, which is coming open in several months.

Your first assignment is to write a report to the hiring committee in which you explain to us the kinds of rhetoric we should look for from those who apply for the position of HC. Before we can hire someone for this position, we have to make sure that our search committee clearly understands what the important features of clear, powerfully persuasive, and smart communication are in the twenty-first century. We expect our new HC to write traditional documents and to create infographics, possibly posters, websites, slide presentations and other print and electronic genres all with the goal of getting nonspecialists excited about making themselves and all those around them truly happy. In your report, please share with the hiring committee texts about happiness that you are familiar with, and explain to them what those texts do effectively and what those texts could do better. After all, we know all about happiness at Happiness, Inc. We hired you to inform us about *composing texts* about happiness that will really help us get our message out.

Good luck; we are all counting on you! Thank you for your help. Stay Happy! ☺

FIGURE 7.2. Ken's pseudo-authentic writing assignment focused on Happiness, Inc.

Midterm Paper Rubric

Midterm papers will be graded according to the following rubric. Paying close attention to the criteria below will help you invent and compose a paper that effectively satisfies the two rhetorical situations your paper must address. Some details have been filled in, but please take time in class to think through details for boxes not filled in and discuss other features of excellent work in each category.

	Excellent	Very Good	Fair	Needs Improvement
Report makes **substantial claims** about the rhetorical effectiveness of 2–3 primary texts about Happiness.	The claims result from a synthesis of rhetorical devices from 2–3 primary texts. There is a rationale given for why these claims are important for the purposes of the report.	The claims result from a synthesis of 2–3 primary texts, but tend to analyze the texts separately.	The claims are separate claims about each primary text, but the analyses of the texts are not at all related to each other.	Claims are not made, or they just point out easy, surface features about the texts—claims that don't take advantage of what we have learned about rhetoric in this class.
Report explains **reasons** for claims about primary texts (explains and analyzes), and gives clear, useful examples from the primary texts.				
Report makes substantial reference to **specific, important rhetorical concepts** from secondary texts and concepts from class handouts, slides, and discussion.				
Report writing is professional in **tone** and **register**.				
Report demonstrates **engagement** and **creativity** in the analysis of primary texts, the use of secondary texts, and in the delivery of the information in the report.	Writer seems to care about the information presented to ensure the readers' needs are fulfilled. The document is written to truly help the readers understand. The analysis of the texts is not the same as everyone else's, and interesting, thoughtful points about the primary texts are made. Images, links, and any other features are used creatively to make the report interesting to read and easy to understand. The fact that this report is for a company invested in Happiness is obvious in many ways in the report.			
Report attends to issues of **delivery**: e.g., the report follows required word count (1500–2500 words), is edited appropriately in standardized English, follows MLA format for citation.	Report looks very professional, has few if any surface errors, and it follows all requirements listed in both pages of the assignment sheets.			

FIGURE 7.3. Rubric for the midterm paper.

Not all assignments have to be so complex, but Ken's assignment shows the kind of creative fun that all of us as veteran teachers can build into our writing assignments. Such innovations can also shift student and class discussions about writing from dry consideration of rules, rights, and wrongs to more sophisticated discussions of strategies, suggestions, and experiments.

ADDING AUTHENTIC CRITERIA TO WRITING RUBRICS

Not every writing teacher is a fan of rubrics. (For some good arguments against using rubrics, see works by Kohn; Wilson; and Thomas. For some excellent work favoring rubrics, see works by Andrade and by Steineke.) We find rubrics useful as long as they help to demystify grading for students and as long as they don't create a formula that hems students in to an inauthentic situation in which they are just filling in blanks and not really composing. We also like rubrics that are created by teachers and students together because such rubrics reflect shared decision making. (And if you are interested in more information on these aspects of rubrics, please consult "Writing, Revising, and Publishing" in Christenbury and Lindblom, *Making the Journey,* 4th ed.)

Regardless of the back and forth about rubric creation and its positive and negative aspects, we also want to focus on rubrics as a way to direct students' attention to the audiences for whom they are writing. Admittedly, in most ways, we as teachers are not real audiences because:

- We are paid to read students' writing.

- We generally set the rules for the writing, and our preferences, biases, and idiosyncrasies influence or even dictate those rules.

- We often know more about the subject the students are writing about than they do, often because we've read hundreds and hundreds of essays from people a lot like them on exactly the same topic.

However, we teachers are real audiences in some ways too. We have preferences as readers, we can be stimulated, we can be moved, surprised, delighted, annoyed, challenged, entertained. In fact, given how much student writing we are required to read, we are grateful to student writing that treats us as a real audience—at least sometimes.

Once, a few years ago, Ken was reading a stack of papers and thought, "Man, I wish these papers were more interesting!" Then it hit him: students will work on what's listed on a rubric. In his next paper assignment, he added this to the rubric: "*Is Interesting to Read.*"

From that point on, his students' papers in general began to get much more enjoyable to read. Students were adding humor or compelling emotional statements, photos, comics, memes, and other creative touches. The students added dialogue and quoted from more interesting sources. They discovered that Word has templates that make a paper a more appealing-looking document.

This change didn't happen overnight, and it didn't happen without working with students. When students see a criterion like "*Is Interesting to Read,*" they need to think and talk about what that means to different audiences. They need to explore, as Aristotle might put it, the available means of interesting readers.

There are at least two advantages to adding the "*Is Interesting to Read*" criterion to rubrics:

▸ It focuses students on some real-world aspects of writing, taking into account that audiences are real people who need to be enticed in some way to read their work.

▸ Students appreciate this skill as something they know will be valuable to them later in their lives. Learning ways to engage real people is something everyone can find useful.

And, as a third advantage, it's impossible to oversell how wonderful it is to read student papers that are genuinely interesting!

This would be a good time to take a walk over to our Teachers' Lounge to see if someone there could give us more ideas for getting real audience feedback on our students' writing. We're in luck! Dawn Reed, high school English teacher and co-director of the Red Cedar Writing Project at Michigan State University, is having a quick snack in between classes, and she's got loads of ideas for us.

FROM THE TEACHERS' LOUNGE

Authentic Audiences Offer Authentic Feedback

Dawn Reed
Okemos High School, Okemos, Michigan

Without a doubt, engagement in authentic learning and opportunities for feedback beyond a teacher or a peer or two is essential for my students' learning. When they write for real audiences, my students make comments like these:

My work is . . .

- *a piece that needs to be good if I am going to share it with someone other than my teacher*
- *more important to me when many people will look at it . . . including people I do not know*
- *a piece that matters*
- *composed for a purpose that is more than* just *for an assignment*
- *part of an important conversation*

There are numerous ways that I incorporate feedback from various audiences. In class, students share writing with one another and through platforms for online discussion, such as Google Classroom discussion forums or other online spaces.

Students also share writing through Youth Voices (https://www .youthvoices.live/), which offers youth a place to publish and respond to other youth from coast to coast. My students in Michigan, for instance, have received comments on their ideas from students in Utah, California, New York, Colorado, Pennsylvania, and other states. In turn, my students respond to students from other schools.

When students research in my class, they may also share research questions and surveys with the Youth Voices community, or we explore opportunities for students to interview people in the community. In both these instances, the conversations around ideas offer students feedback relevant to the aims of their writing and learning.

Students engage in composing projects related to engagement with the world around us. Educational partners offer powerful education connections for students to compose for audiences beyond themselves, such as through collaborations with local or online news sources. KQED Education (https://ww2.kqed.org/education/), for example, offers several educational invitations for teachers and students to engage in work with a larger audience and has been a support for my students and my teaching for a number of years.

Additionally, on Letters to the Next President 2.0 (https://letters2 president.org/), students composed pieces for the 2016 presidential election highlighting issues they researched and deemed important for our next president of the United States to consider. During the 2017–18 school year, students shared responses to the PBS documentary American Creed *on the Writing Our Future (https://writingourfuture.nwp.org/american creed) space. These pieces are still receiving feedback from others through conversation in our local community and from national conversations sparked through partners such as PBS and the National Writing Project in blogs and on Twitter.*

In each opportunity, students are invited to write beyond the classroom so that they can enter into a conversation, receiving more than a grade and focusing on ideas and the discussion surrounding their writing. In this way, authentic opportunities for feedback support students in their authentic compositions and engagement in issues relevant to our lives today.

CONCLUSION: TEACHING WRITING IS NOT A ONE-PERSON JOB

Learning to write is a lot like learning to teach: you can prepare to learn to do it in theory, but the only way to really learn how to do it is by really doing it.

As writing teachers, we need to immerse our students in the world of real writing, not just engage them in the kinds of formal, academic writing that are most often taught and most often tested. And we believe the best way to immerse students in real writing is to have them write to real audiences for real purposes and in real contexts. That means even we very talented veteran writing teachers can't (and shouldn't) teach writing on our own. To truly teach our students, we must find ways to harness outside audiences for our students' writing. To complete the cycle, we must also ensure that our students are invested in the responses of those real audiences by counting those responses in final grades.

Rather than being a burden, we often find that working with outside audiences brings an energy and enthusiasm into our classrooms that makes the experience more exciting and easier for all of us, students and teachers.

Teaching Language in the Context of Authentic Writing Instruction

THE AUDIENCE RULES

Authentic writing instruction makes teaching writing more interesting and more fun, but it also makes it more complicated. There is one area, however, that authentic writing can make simpler for English teachers: what counts as correct language. In authentic writing, the audience rules and is also judge, jury, and executioner—because the audience determines what will be executed: the writer's goal or the writer's writing. Real audiences can choose whether to follow the writer's wishes or ignore the writer altogether.

To illustrate what can be quite a conundrum in writing, here's an example adapted from a section of *Grammar Rants* (Dunn and Lindblom) titled "The Grammar Trap" (94):

Each person should bring _____ best idea to the meeting.

What's the correct answer to fill in the blank?

To answer this question, some people might suggest consulting a handbook, but even respected handbooks differ in their responses. Some people might offer *his* as the answer (what was once termed the "generic" or "universal" gender). Many might find that choice sexist and suggest instead a more inclusive term, such as *his or her*. Others might find that too wordy and suggest a bolder but increasingly accepted gender-neutral term: *their* (using *they* as a singular). Still others might prefer a less wordy, nonsexist term that doesn't break traditional subject-agreement conventions, such as *his/her* (this also gives rise to a similar form: *s/he*). But some readers detest a slash.

So what is correct?

A traditional writing teacher might just pick one variation and go with it. Other teachers might throw up their hands and complain about the decline of English language mores and Western civilization along with it! (We've both spent time in that frustrated territory.)

But a teacher of authentic writing has a clear answer that also happens to have the benefit of being true: the correct answer is *what your audience will consider correct.*

So think about *who* you are writing to, and fill in the blank in the way that would fulfill your purpose with that audience. Chances are you don't want to distract (or puzzle or especially offend) your audience, so you might select the answer least likely to even be noticed. But to do that, you need to think about your audience's beliefs.

The audience rules and is King.

Or Queen.

Or King/Queen.

Or Monarch.

WHAT IT MEANS TO PRIORITIZE AUDIENCE

How do we help developing writers understand how to make decisions that prioritize their audiences? When questions of language use arise in writing, especially during the editing and proofreading stages of writing processes, how do we treat language in a way that takes audience seriously?

The answer to these questions is, again, pretty simple: give students lots and lots of experience writing in many genres and for many purposes and for many different real audiences.

When you have an authentic approach to teaching language, you are no longer the sole arbiter of your students' correctness. These concerns, and others like them, become paramount:

- What is the context of the communication? Formal, informal?

- What is the relationship of the writer to the reader? Is there a hierarchy of authority?

- In what medium is the communication taking place? An oral presentation, a letter, a social media post?

Now, you—like a linguist—can allow the world around you, including the context of the specific communication, to help your students learn about what works and what doesn't work in English Language. Sure there are rules to be observed and lessons to be learned, but it's not about correction; it's about facilitation. Correction is for changing behavior, for pointing out a fault to be forever avoided in the future. Facilitation is about changing a mindset, about getting someone to think more critically, in a more informed manner.

It might bring the matter more solidly home to closely examine the word *correction* and its meanings as listed in the *Oxford English Dictionary*:

- The action of correcting or setting right; substitution of what is right for what is erroneous in (a book, etc.); amendment. Hence, loosely, pointing out or marking of errors (in order to their removal).

- *under correction*: subject to correction; a formula expressing deference to superior information, or critical authority.

- (with *a* and *pl.*) An act or instance of emendation; *concr.* that which is substituted for what is wrong or faulty, *esp.* in a literary work; an emendation.

- The correcting (of a person) for faults of character or conduct; reprehension, rebuke, reproof.

- The correcting (of a person) by disciplinary punishment; chastisement, properly with a view to amendment; but frequently in later use (now somewhat *arch.*) of corporal punishment, flogging.

Do you see it as your job to remove linguistically appropriate language from your students' repertoires? Are you requiring them to defer to a superior? Are you eradicating faults of character, punishing, chastising? Is this the tradition you are working from as a teacher?

You may be, whether you know it or not. But we trust you prefer not to.

MORALITY AND STANDARDIZED ENGLISH

There are many theories as to why so many people still believe that standardized English is the one and only proper English, even in the face of decades, perhaps a century, of descriptive linguistics that shows otherwise. Why does this reverence for standardized English persist? Is it tradition? Habit? Or something more insidious?

Most bad—or, to be direct, inaccurate—writing and language instruction comes from the fact that it is based in a theory of language that was created some centuries ago when "correct" or "proper" English came to be a marker not of communicative excellence but of class status. We can thank Samuel Johnson and his very first English dictionary for codifying what was, at the time, a rather Wild West of English pronunciation and spelling. Johnson's dictionary put in place some standards and regulations for the language. That, of course, was the good news, but the bad news is that Johnson's work and subsequent English rule books then came to be seen as a language etiquette book of sorts, and often the "rules" bore little relation to reality (one infamous example is the "rule" against split infinitives, a totally artificial prohibition based on the supposed superiority of Latin—which has a one-word infinitive—to the two-word infinitive in English).

When, without any kind of context, we maintain these "rules," the purpose of such instruction is then not to teach people to be effective communicators, but instead to instill in them a version of English Language that some powerful others rather arbitrarily consider correct. English becomes some poor Frankensteinian confabulation built from used parts of old languages combined with the language habits of people in power. Presumably experts, these dominant others establish regulations that are to be followed like sets of directions to enable any form of communication anywhere. And if that "correct" communication doesn't work, it's a fault of the audience, who either doesn't know any better or doesn't care. Departures from these rules can be used at any time by the powerful to demonstrate the prima facie unworthiness of the author or speakers whose words don't conform. (We see this constantly, especially on social media: "How can I take your argument seriously when you don't even know the difference before *your* and *you're*?") This is entirely unjust, and it quietly but powerfully props up discriminatory practices that ensure an insidiously unfair linguistic playing field. We veteran writing teachers can and should push past this dishonest parody of real language.

Ken and his colleague Patricia A. Dunn examine what is behind people's eagerness to judge and correct others based on their use of language:

> One possible reason for bad grammar's association with bad morals is the perceived connection between error and laziness. . . . People who make mistakes in grammar are often considered to be tasteless, contemptuous of authority, but most of all lazy. Perhaps it is the perceived laziness that [grammar] ranters connect with one of the seven deadly sins in Christianity: sloth. (1–2)

Some people feel compelled to correct or simply enjoy correcting other people's language use. English teachers are not only encouraged to indulge this urge, but also are often *expected* to correct every departure from standardized English. For some reason, Leila is dogged by these correctness questions in much of her social circle: parties to which she is invited become a trial when she is cornered about language issues, the deterioration of other people's speech, and a general lament about literacy. And these are the adults!

But, as we discuss throughout this book, to help *students* learn to use language effectively, we must resist the urge to correct. Instead we must develop more open and accurate understandings of literacy and language.

Our goal as English teachers should be to assist students in becoming confident, effective users of English Language in all its forms. Correction won't get them there. Authentic experience and reflection will.

We urge you to make sure students have many opportunities to experience the real-world results of their and other students' attempts to achieve purposes in writing. In doing this, students will learn what really works, what doesn't work, when things work, and when they don't.

As veteran teachers, our role is to act as guides, mentors, and fellow analysts, helping students to succeed in their writing, and learning what happened when their writing did or did not work. Writing for the real world is challenging, and much as we might not like it or feel comfortable about it, the rules of language and correctness are not as clean and clear as in most writing reference books. In fact, writing for real audiences can challenge a great deal of what we may teach about Standard English, or what we more accurately prefer to call *standardized* English.

Being a successful communicator requires understanding and wielding different forms and rules of English in different contexts. If your students leave you believing there is only one "good" or "correct" language—whether or not it's the language they grew up speaking and writing—you are hamstringing their future abilities to communicate effectively with people. Many of us—including Ken and Leila—were raised to speak and write one "proper English" and to eschew anything else. This is embedded in our ideas, our attitudes, even our identity expression. So are we destined to misserve our students? What's the alternative?

To serve our students' futures effectively, we must develop more accurate ways of presenting our understanding of English Language, and allow that more accurate understanding to infuse our writing instruction, particularly in the latter stages of editing and in questions of correctness.

Here are the things we know from research and experience to be true about English Language and writers:

- There is no one, correct English Language. Rather, English Language takes multiple forms that function in various, even competing, ways in different contexts.

- Rules of all forms of English Language change over time. New words are coined, old words become outdated, and new grammatical constructions develop and function effectively.

▸ Effective communicators of English Language change the form of English they use frequently, often using more than one form of English in the same day, and sometimes even using different forms of English in the same communication.

▸ To be truly effective users of English Language, communicators must determine what form(s) of English Language will be most effective for them to use at any given time for any given purpose with any given audience.

▸ In any given situation, there are forms of English Language that would be considered ineffective, even incorrect. Communicators must be able to identify these and be able to avoid them or to accept any consequences.

▸ Many formal written forums have editorial boards that are well aware of the multiplicity of forms of correct English, and thus they have established language style guides to create a standardized set of conventions, frequently called a "house style" for that forum (a magazine or newspaper, a company, a university). These guides are regularly updated to keep current with contemporary language shifts and needs. For example, check out the editorial style guide for Stony Brook University: https://www.stonybrook.edu/brand/content/editorial-style-guide/. The *New York Times* publishes its inhouse style guide, now in its fifth edition (Siegal and Connolly).

▸ People's identities are shot through with the ways in which they were taught to communicate. Teaching a single form of English as if it is inherently better, smarter, more correct, or in any way superior is to discriminate among students' identities, teaching them to think less (or more) of themselves than is justified. This is not just about spelling and punctuation and vocabulary: it is an important matter of accuracy and of social justice.

▸ Learning to be an effective communicator requires a great deal of experience writing and speaking with a wide range of real communicators, real audiences, real purposes, and real contexts. And it requires a great deal of reflecting on how English Language actually works in real-world interactions.

Prioritizing audience and also divorcing language from a spurious link to morality means being open as a writing teacher to all forms of written communication, and understanding that different conventions operate among different communities—or sometimes even in the same communities at different times. Writers must experience these differences, engage in them with agency and autonomy, and feel, to at least a certain degree, the consequences both positive and negative of the choices they make as writers in those different communities. That means working in a context of authentic language.

THE PLACE OF STANDARDIZED ENGLISH

Before we move on, let's take care of some important business right off. Let's be exceptionally clear and direct: teaching language in an authentic manner *does not* mean avoiding reality, i.e., the position and the power of standardized English.

In fact, all students must learn that in many places, particularly places in which they have limited power, they will be expected to effectively use standardized English correctly, and not using standardized English correctly is likely to cause them significant problems. We want to be very clear about this, as we are both pragmatists: *students must learn to use standardized English*. Standardized English is most often the default prestige dialect, what Geneva Smitherman has called "the language of wider communication" (*Talkin* 1977). Teaching students conventions of standardized English, at least to some extent, enables their social mobility and prepares them to succeed in most professional contexts. We explore this later, especially as we discuss the importance of students changing and moving among language registers, a facility that can help them in every aspect of their personal and professional lives.

But students must also learn that standardized English is not inherently superior to any other form of English Language that effectively carries meaning from one person to another. Taught as a powerful, not a necessarily better, version of English, standardized English is an important part of being an effective communicator of English Language.

DEVELOPING A DISPOSITION TO TEACH WRITING AUTHENTICALLY

Some attitudes and ideas that many of us have been taught about language are completely inconsistent with an authentic approach to teaching writing. In some ways, becoming a better teacher of writing may require unlearning those attitudes and ideas. Following are some concepts to think about.

"ENGLISH LANGUAGE" VS. "*THE* ENGLISH LANGUAGE"

This first request may seem a bit unusual, but we ask that you try to remove the phrase "*the* English Language" from your repertoire, instead preferring "English Language" without the *the*. If you think about it, *the* implies that there is one form of correct English, and that just isn't true. In fact, the inaccuracy in the use of *the* interferes with writers' abilities to engage readers effectively because *the* encourages a too-narrow approach to what is a colorful, living palette of language possibilities within English. When you use *the*, you prop up a whole problematic system of language that exists only because some people (and linguists might identify these people as both conservatives and elitists) keep propping it up.

The language we call English is actually a set of different global versions of English, such as (and each one of these titles is also inadequate to capture the nuances of language variations) informal English, African American English, working-class English, Appalachian English, rural English, Bronx English, Australian English, Indian English, British English, and, yes, standardized English. If you're teaching *the* English Language, as opposed to English Language, you may already be trapped in an English Language laboratory, in which you learn, identify, and teach rules that don't function in the world outside that lab.

Move out of that laboratory and get some fresh air! Breathe in the many varied and creative ways in which English is used to communicate. Teach living versions of English, not some dead body of rules, tacked to a table like a petrified moth in a natural history museum. In a word, teach *authentic* English: the multiform English that shifts in tone, organization, and content to meet the needs of each context, audience, and purpose.

STANDARD*IZED* ENGLISH VS. STANDARD ENGLISH

Much like adding the *the* above, leaving out the *-ized* in *standardized* English also belies a truth about language: Standard English is no more inherently correct than any other form of English that accurately transmits knowledge from a writer to a reader. But leaving out the *-ized* perpetuates the myth that standardized English is somehow inherently better than other forms of English, and ipso facto, those who use it are better people. Leaving out the *-ized* allows partial, elitist views of language to operate on "the down-low," as Keith Gilyard, Edwin Erle Sparks Professor at Penn State University and former chair of NCTE's Conference on College Composition and Communication, observed almost twenty years ago:

> [T]he use of the term Standard English as opposed to Standardized English makes it seem like the standard variety dropped from the clouds ([Clark and Ivanič] 211). Get that *IZE* up in there and you can focus more on the fact that the standardIZED variety was selected by the linguistic elite. And this standardIZED variety is packed with all this down-low elite material. (267)

As we discussed earlier, standardized English isn't a bad thing. It's a necessary and important concept in the teaching of writing. Students must learn to wield standardized English deftly so they can use it effectively *when* they decide to use it.

But we should also let students in on the secret that standardized English didn't come from the gods' lips to our ears. The codified rules of standardized English come from books, and those books change with the times, and, further, many of them don't agree with each other on what standardized English conventions are. In many ways, each piece of writing is an educated guess about what will be counted as correct in any rhetorical situation. Helping students to become good educated guessers means letting them in on all this deep background.

EMPLOY STYLE AND USAGE GUIDES

All serious writers and editors use style and usage guides to help them communicate effectively. These are not grammar handbooks, although they often include information about grammar. Instead, they offer broader information on more nuanced questions in using English. A great favorite of ours is *Garner's Modern American Usage: The Authority on Grammar, Usage, and Style,* 3rd ed. Garner brings his considerable knowledge about English to an examination of an enormous corpus of published American writing to make judgments on questions of language use for American audiences. He lays out empirical evidence gathered from published material across the spectrum of American publications, gives his own opinion (stated as just that: his opinion), and even makes educated guesses about how departures from previously held conventions might go over with different audiences; some departures might be considered "refined," others no worse than "elbows on a table," still others, though, would be like "audible farting" (xxxv). When should you use *which* or *that*? Can I use *till* in writing, or should it always be *until*? Should I describe someone in her seventies as *elderly* or a *senior*? Can *impact* be used as a verb? A good usage manual can be a godsend when those picky questions come up—and when we're able to get students to truly care about the outcomes of their writing, they will come up!

HONOR THE LANGUAGE HERITAGE OF THE STUDENTS WE TEACH

As we teach writing, we should follow the precepts of culturally relevant pedagogy by treating our students as people of unique experience and identity. According to Winn and Johnson, doing so:

> command[s] a certain disposition—one that can regard students as experts, one that is open to learning about the lives of students, and one that can push students to connect their lives to the world around them. . . . [Culturally relevant pedagogy] welcomes students' voices, demands their reflection, and pushes them toward discovery of the self. (14)

Honoring the languages our students bring with them to our classrooms is part of the job of authentic writing instruction. Let students who are native speakers of languages other than English or standardized English write to their native audiences in those languages, and ask them to translate what they've written into English for the teacher and other students. Let them draft in their home languages or dialects. If those drafts must be edited into standardized English during a later stage in their writing processes, so be it. Treat standardized English as *an addition* to the other languages your students bring to class. Don't try to eliminate the other languages students bring with them. As we hope we have argued persuasively in this chapter, other languages and other versions of English are assets, not deficits.

Teaching from a deficit model—that is, treating every student's departure from standardized English as a negative—can have drastic implications. Such a pedagogy can reinforce harmful myths invisibly, as Gilyard puts it, "on the down-low." In a particularly extreme and disturbing case, composition scholars Min-Zahn Lu and Bruce Horner describe a horrific trend among some Asian communities in which doctors, upon request, surgically remove the frenulum (the small strip of flesh under the tongue) from children and adults to make it easier for them to reduce their accent when they speak English (99). Lu and Horner caution teachers to take care in "imply[ing] a consensus among all users of English that only one way of using English counts as accent free and thus proper or good" (99). Yes, this is an extreme trend, but it is one logical if ill-conceived extension of uninterrogated assumptions about "proper" English.

As veteran teachers, we need to ensure that we are teaching language accurately and effectively. We should teach critical thought and effective communication, not bias and unexamined assumption, even inadvertently. Because language is so intimately connected to identity, teaching the former is inextricably linked to the latter. Language is personal, and writing teachers need to take care to teach it in a just manner.

Well, it's time for a break and a visit to our Teachers' Lounge. Lorena Germán, a Texas high school teacher and 2014 NCTE Early Career Educator of Color Leadership Award recipient, takes the language backgrounds of her students seriously in her teaching. Germán has freed up some time from her busy teaching schedule to visit our Teachers' Lounge, where she shares some of her ideas with us.

--- FROM THE TEACHERS' LOUNGE ---

Teaching Language, Teaching Justice

Lorena Germán
Headwaters School, Austin, Texas

My teaching experience ranges from a predominantly Latinx public classroom setting to a predominantly White private school. I've adjusted what I've taught and the way I've taught it based on my context and who was sitting in front of me. One challenge I've faced: encouraging students to be open to various forms of English language. Driving home the notion that Dominant American English isn't the only valid English; that entire communities practice other Englishes; that this variety builds on the richness of this country, has not been an easy task. One important place to start is having conversations about language and its power.

My students and I have discussed the ways language is weaponized and used to achieve and maintain status. We talk about how English is taught and how that learning is privileged. We discuss the ways that vernacular indexes race and class in The Adventures of Huckleberry Finn, *for example. We read and discuss James Baldwin's "If Black English Isn't a Language, Then Tell Me, What Is?" and its implications in the English classroom. We compare and contrast the English language present in* To Kill a Mockingbird *and* The Hate U Give, *and language's role in the White gaze. Caliban in Shakespeare's* The Tempest *is also a great character for our exploration, specifically when he identifies the way his colonizer's English was a tool for oppression, while all he can use it for is cursing. We also read excerpts of Rigoberta Menchú's* I, Rigoberta Menchú *and analyze her use of Spanish, the colonizer's language, in her exposition, and we made connections to the use of English language.*

It is essential for teachers of literacy to consider the ways that our profession must shift along with our country. As we think of the changing demographics of our classroom and the truth of our nation's history on this soil, we have a responsibility to prepare our students to interact respectfully with this world. I believe my students learned many lessons in these units and conversations that went beyond the traditional academic objectives. I know I learned some important ones. I learned that students are ready to engage in these conversations, but they need a space. I also learned that my content area isn't separate from justice; it's not separate from the work of dismantling oppression. It is at the core.

We have another visitor to our Teachers' Lounge. Y'Shanda Young-Rivera, a former teacher now at Northwestern University, is coauthor of an important book on language teaching: *Other People's English: Code-Meshing, Code-Switching, and African American Literacy.* Like Germán, Young-Rivera takes students' identities into serious account as she teaches writing. Enjoying a cup of tea and a rare moment of relaxation in our Teachers' Lounge, she fills us in on her thinking.

FROM THE TEACHERS' LOUNGE

Valuing Students' Language Repertoires:
An Ecological Perspective

Y'Shanda Young-Rivera
Northwestern University, Evanston, Illinois

Let's begin with a writing exercise. Take thirty seconds to make a list of the people/places that have influenced who you are. Now notice who/what is on your list. Take a few minutes to detail how these persons/places influenced you.

Take another to reflect. As you were writing, did you find yourself smiling, laughing, frowning, or even crying? Ask yourself, Why?

<u>*You*</u>*: A complex individual shaped by various social, cultural, historical, political, and ideological influences and interactions.*

<u>*Students*</u>*: Complex individuals shaped by various social, cultural, historical, political, and ideological influences and interactions.*

This brief writing performance helps to advance my major point: language and literacy teachers should help students develop as writers and speakers from an ecological perspective. Bronfenbrenner's ecological system theory (EST) (Ecology; Making) outlines how a child's development is influenced by multiple systems on multiple levels. A child's overall development doesn't happen in isolation and neither does their linguistic development. An ecological approach asks students to recognize and draw from multifaceted micro- and macro-level influences in their lives, positioning and empowering them with agency to reflect relevant aspects of themselves, in both formal and informal, oral and written assignments.

As I apply an EST frame to my students' language repertoires, I must acknowledge the language practices and habits from the multiple "systems" in their lives. Rather than treating these practices and habits as factors that need to be separated and parsed out from their "school selves," I aim to create a harmonious interaction among them. I encourage you to do the same.

Here's why.

Prominent linguists such as Geneva Smitherman (Talkin), Mary Rhodes Hoover, and Rosina Lippi-Green have exposed the long-held secret that Standard English (SE) arises only from a set of school-based grammar rules. These scholars argue that students' (and professionals') use of SE will and should demonstrate and reflect influences from their lives. For instance, Hoover advances the term Black Standard English *to* encourage Black students to draw on their African American language heritages at all times, including in formal and school contexts (69). When Black and Brown students are kept from using an ecological approach in their development as effective readers, speakers, and writers, they are being robbed of their identities. They are not permitted to be who they are. Unfortunately, this has been a sad reality of formal literacy instruction in schools. As teachers, dare we foreground a new narrative?

Let us strengthen our students' literacies, ecologically, through code-meshing. Let's teach them the works of Toni Morrison (1988 Pulitzer Prize winner; 1993 Nobel Prize in Literature winner), Ta-Nehisi Coates (2015 National Book Award winner), Junot Díaz (2008 Pulitzer Prize winner), and Sandra Cisneros (1985 American Book Award winner), individuals whose blended language repertoires, in speaking and writing, earned them national and international awards.

Let us show them A. D. Carson, a Clemson University 2017 PhD graduate in mass communication, whose dissertation was a thirty-four-song hip-hop album that won him Clemson's Graduate Student Outstanding Dissertation award.

Let us show them Kendrick Lamar, whose 2018 Pulitzer Prize–winning Damn. is described as "a virtuosic song collection unified by its vernacular authenticity . . . that offers affecting vignettes capturing the complexity of modern African-American life" (http://www.pulitzer.org/winners/kendrick-lamar).

Let us show that we value our students' language repertoires by providing them extensive opportunities to code-mesh through freewriting, debates, storytelling, various digital media platforms, and yes, formal written essays also (Smitherman, "Blacker"; Young).

Let us set students free to smile, laugh, frown, and cry as they reflect and write with words that intricately intertwine their multifaceted selves.

And let us too, along with all of society, be linguistically richer because of it.

INCORPORATE CODE-MESHING ASSIGNMENTS

Code-meshing assignments allow students to write in more than one style, dialect, or register (level of formality) of English in a single communication. Code-meshing scholar and advocate Vershawn Ashanti Young asks, why shouldn't we allow "students and professionals to merge their Englishes, to produce the best prose from a combination of all their language resources?" (Young, Barrett, Young-Rivera, and Lovejoy 5). A sentence we cited earlier in this chapter from Keith Gilyard about standardized English is an example of code-meshing: "Get that *IZE* up in there and you can focus more on the fact that the standardIZED variety was selected by the linguistic elite" (267). This essay was based on a keynote speech Gilyard gave at the Conference on College Composition and Communication Annual Convention (NCTE's organization for college writing teachers), and Ken was there to hear the speech.

 **PROFESSOR GILYARD DELIVERED** *his speech to a packed house at the conference, hundreds of people. He is a commanding speaker and quickly had most of the audience in the palm of his hand. Throughout his keynote address, he slipped in and out of traditional academic-sounding discourse. Because part of the point he was making was that our language practices come in a social and political context and that theorizing these contexts can enrich writing instruction, his use of multiple versions of English in his talk was not only an example of code-meshing but also a vivid point in its favor. The audience was rapt, and Gilyard's ideas came across as more authentic, more compelling, and more obviously right because of his use of multi-*

ple dialects and registers. For most readers of the essay revised from his speech, this is almost certainly still the case.

Y'Shanda Young-Rivera, whom we met just a few minutes ago in our Teachers' Lounge, also published about her work on two different code-meshing lessons with classes in Chicago: a class of Latinx bilingual students in grades 4–5 and a class of grade 8 students, half of whom were African American and the other half Latinx.

The grades 4–5 students used English and Spanish together in their assignments. For example, the teacher would put English words on the board and then ask the students for the Spanish equivalents. Interestingly, the teacher then asked the students why they hadn't chosen other Spanish words, words she knew were more formal or were from regional dialects of Spanish that the students didn't use themselves. This allowed the students and the teacher to discuss register, regionalism, and other linguistic concepts in relation to Spanish and English Language (Young, Barrett, Young-Rivera, and Lovejoy 104). By contrast, the grade 8 students engaged in a debate about the use of code-meshing in school. First the teacher introduced the concept of code-meshing by asking students to bring in examples of code-meshing from music lyrics; the students found lots of examples from artists they admired (98–99). Then she had the students engage in in-depth assignments to prepare them for a debate on the topic, for which they were assigned sides: pro or con. In the end, the students were invited to give their own thoughts in a discursive survey (108–9).

Young-Rivera's experience inclined her to see code-meshing as promising because it "meets students where they are, validates who they are, and exposes them to new experiences, which in turn enhances who they become" (Young et al. 117). She bases this conclusion on several observations she made during the code-meshing activities. She saw:

1.   Students who felt free to write and express themselves, using words of their own choosing.

2.   Students who had no inhibitions and weren't fearful that what they wrote would be wrong.

3. Students who felt empowered, so much so that I even think some of them were deliberately using their dialect speech patterns, just because they could. (111)

Although our examples of code-meshing come from classrooms in which the students were primarily students of color and/or English language learners, White students who are native English speakers also benefit from code-meshing assignments that validate their backgrounds. Students from working-class backgrounds could use the speech patterns of their vernacular, and all students could employ regionalisms or informal rhetorical registers in their writing in ways that might allow them to see their full backgrounds as legitimate parts of their identities as writers. Think about forms of English common in eastern Kentucky, New Orleans, South Side Chicago, East St. Louis, West Texas, and so on.

For too long, learning to write for some students has meant years of being told that the ways and language of their families and others in their culture are wrong, are somehow less than those who grew up with standardized English as their primary discourse. Students will be better writers—and more authentic writers—if we treat their backgrounds as a resource, not as refuse.

CONCLUSION: MEETING THE CHALLENGE OF AUTHENTIC WRITING INSTRUCTION

Learning to write effectively in English is a challenging task, one that nobody ever truly masters. Taking on the task of teaching others to write effectively takes a gargantuan amount of moxie, a hood to pull over one's eyes to hide the enormity of the task, or an approach that enlists the very complexity of English Language to immerse students in the vast task. Throughout this book, we choose the third option. Our approach can be summed up in one, modest word with a mountain behind it: *authenticity*.

Our students and our world face real, significant issues, and our authentic writing instruction demands that we respond. That response is part of our continuing journey as veteran teachers of English. That journey is long and sometimes difficult. When we stray from the well-worn path, we sometimes stumble and get rocks in our shoes. In those cases, we stop momentarily, deal with the challenge, and take the next step to more and more interesting, beautiful, and worthwhile territory ahead.

Authenticity Today: Writing the Real

The childhood chant, *Sticks and stones can break my bones / But words can never hurt me,* is one of the more egregious lies found in our cultural storehouse of folk wisdom. The words we speak and write can indeed hurt, cut, demean, and at times even annihilate. Words create images, connote tone, and indicate register. Words form poetic phrases and harsh commands. They weave meaningful conversations, express deep emotions, explain difficult propositions. Words can be funny or clinical, clear or ambiguous. They can be rude or polite, targeted to a specific audience or designed for broad understanding. Language can be obvious and sincere, or coded and ironic. In a negative context, words can be used to disguise the truth and to demonize the enemy. They can also, as we the English teacher lovers of writing and language know, inspire, comfort, and lead us to be far better individuals than we had ever imagined. Words can wound, but they can also advance societies and change lives.

For the religious, words in sacred texts guide a life; for the nonreligious, words in secular texts do the same. For some, the 23rd Psalm from the Bible ("The Lord is my shepherd") is a touchstone; for others, the opening lines of the US Declaration of Independence ("We hold these truths to be self-evident") holds a similar significance. The oft-quoted (famously by Dr. Martin Luther King, Jr.) "The arc of the moral universe is long, but it bends toward justice" gives many confidence to continue work to make a better society.

And we don't need to spend extraordinary time detailing the history of the use and misuse of writing and language to make a case in our classrooms that words have unique power. Our students know—and use—such words in their own lives, and words promote what they love and treasure, what they disrespect and what they scorn. For adults, for young people, for teachers, and for students, "Words are tools, and what matters is the job that they are being made to do" (Menand 16).

For us as teachers of authentic writing and language, the richness of words is all around us, and we need look no further than the daily news feed for a treasure of literacy instruction. This of course does not mean that we abandon consideration of classic texts and phrases. How and why "the better angels of our nature" (Abraham Lincoln, *First Inaugural Address*); "[I]t is wrong to use immoral means to attain moral ends. . . . [I]t is just as wrong, or even more, to use moral means to preserve immoral ends" (Martin Luther King Jr., *Letter from Birmingham Jail*); "[S]o we beat on, boats against the current, borne back ceaselessly into the past" (F. Scott Fitzgerald, *The Great Gatsby*) work and move us is a legitimate topic of English class.

But if we care about relevant and authentic instruction of writing and language, we can also look at today's tweets and sound bites and ask our students to consider the power of words that are now, as much as at any time in our recent history, "weaponized" (Menand 16). We can, for instance, examine what is termed *weak*, what is *fake*, what is *woke*, what is *politically correct,* who feels he or she is a *snowflake, w*ho gets to determine whose form of *patriotism* is genuine. We can consider with our students how a social movement can emerge, often based on memes or slogans that have captured the public imagination (#MeToo; #BlackLivesMatter; #Time'sUp; #NeverAgain).

Regardless of political persuasion, this is the current conversation; our students are aware of it, and we can bring it into our teaching and into our classrooms with confidence. As veteran teachers, we can negotiate these conversations with far more assurance and facility than many of our less experienced colleagues.

We ask students to *write the real* when we ask them to be authentic in their writing. We can fight back against what a nationally distributed essay from a college teacher of first-year writing describes as students who are fearful of using *I* in their essays. A veteran instructor, Scott Korb frets that these students—clearly, students who we have taught in high school—fear that there is nothing in their lives that they value that is truly worthy of writing, that there is nothing that has "earned the right to be heard" (n.p.). Korb notes:

> A decade teaching young writers has taught me a great deal. First, we need to value more the complete and complex lives of young people: where they come from, how they express themselves. They have already lived lives worthy of our attention and appreciation.
>
> Second, we need to encourage young people to take seriously those lives they've lived, even as they come to understand—often through schooling and just as often not—that there's a whole lot more we'll expect of them. Through this, we can help them learn to expect more of themselves, too. (n.p.)

His advice to his own students:

> Look around at what baffles you; look in at your peculiar self and how your own frontiers continue to edge back. Don't worry, you'll never fully grasp how the world transcends you and your ability to describe it. I surely don't, and I'm 41! But don't forget: You've been trying to understand and triumph in the world for as long as you can remember, even as a kid. Now go and write. (SR11)

THE WRITING PRACTICE OF VETERAN TEACHERS

This advice is heeded by effective veteran teachers who invite their students to write the real. Two vignettes from recent classroom observations illustrate this in practice.

Vignette One

The grade 10 honors students in a suburban high school are reading *Night,* a perennial classic often chosen for its high impact, its historical significance, and, not unimportant, its brevity. In this mid-spring class, mostly White, mostly middle-class, largely Christian and suburban students grapple with a classic memoir that recounts events from almost eighty years ago. Significantly for the teacher who is directing this unit, *Night* also details the author's deep belief that some horrific actions are beyond forgiveness.

For this veteran teacher, it's important that her unit on *Night* directly address this concern. In a feel-good era in which reconciliation is often a foregone conclusion, where *hug it out* or *talk it out* is assumed to resolve all conflicts, survivor and author Elie Wiesel is distinctive. In parts of his memoir, Wiesel is almost intransigent about the possibility of forgiveness, and in this class, guided by their teacher, his teenage readers must grapple with that thorny assumption.

Discussing this issue and connecting it to today's ideas, the teacher uses writing to prompt students' consideration of the weighty issues. A mash-up text, taking the lines of *Night* and interleaving them with pertinent poems ("Could Have," Wislawa Szymborska; "Auschwitz," Charles N. Whittaker; "Holocaust," Barbara Sonek; "First They Came . . . ," Martin Niemoller) starts the work, and in groups students create these mash-ups and share them in class. There is further note taking and questions on additional readings as well as a video by Holocaust survivor Eva Mozes Kor to sharpen the focus on different views of forgiveness. The students then complete a journal entry and share with one another, writing down questions they have and circulating the entries so that each student in the class answers others' questions. Only then do students directly tackle the topic of forgiveness and, in the face of implacable destruction and evil, the possibility of reconciliation. The result is a three-page paper that, after submission, becomes, once again, the topic of a large-group discussion.

Observing these classes on *Night* and the use of the writing that students produce, it's clear that many students are not ready or willing to delve as deeply into this topic as the teacher would like. What remains unforgivable is not detailed extensively nor completely "owned" by these tenth graders. Nevertheless, much of the activity in this unit has used writing and readers' responses to the writing to approach this complex issue and to provide for students a way to discuss significant concerns. The threads of discussion have woven material, still thin but perhaps durable, to cover such a weighty topic. This is writing the real.

Vignette Two

It's half an hour into this early morning grade 9 class. The class is in an independent school, and the well-manicured setting is more like a college campus than a secondary school. The student body is tight-knit and largely college bound; the teachers are mostly veterans and comfortable in their classrooms.

Today the teacher asks her fifteen ninth graders to talk in groups. It's January and everyone has just come off a three-day holiday. Somewhat restless but largely attentive, the students perk up at the teacher's unusual directive: "Think of the craziest story that has ever happened to you in or outside class."

Students are invited to turn to a partner and tell that story, and, to make a point that will be more clear later, the teacher steps out of the classroom and stands out of sight in the hall. The students comply quickly and, with their teacher pointedly out of the room, seem to open the conversation and talk excitedly and avidly. After five minutes, the teacher returns to the room and asks the students to take the story they have just told and now to tell it again. But this time, the audience is not each other but, for a change, their grandmother. The students talk to each other for a few minutes, retelling their tales.

The teacher then stops the class and asks students what changed in their stories. (This is a metacognitive move we identify as *triangulation* earlier in this book; see pages 53–56.) Students give multiple answers, and she makes a list on the whiteboard as students share the large and small alterations they spontaneously created. Once the list is about two dozen items long, the teacher stops writing and tells her students to consider this list. What they have done in these two stories, she notes, is to shift *tone* as it relates to *audience*. They may also have altered *content*. The teacher doesn't give the students a definition of the terms, but points again to the differences they have noted that she has reproduced on the whiteboard. Students talk about the items they have contributed, and it's clear they understand, from their own self-selected stories, that they can and do change content and details to fit their audience.

Now it's time to write. The topic is an opinion piece on a social issue, and the students can choose one of two audiences for their writing. One is a nationally known newspaper and one is a popular opinion blog, both of which the class briefly discusses so that students are reminded of what each publication represents and what its audience expects. Whichever forum students choose, they will need, as with their stories, to tailor their comments, and in groups, students begin to discuss the points they will make, what they will say, and how they will say it, for either publication.

These veteran teachers and many others who write with their students every day are forging responsible and responsive discourse; they are providing for their students authentic audiences and instances to write. They are taking the time to let students think through their ideas, to enrich the content of their writing, to try it out on other readers, and to revise their writing based on their initial readers' reactions and what they learn from other students' drafts. These veteran teachers are not giving definitions and assuming students will make the connection: they are asking students to write about important issues and to take stands, to labor until they find an angle that is of real interest to them. Finally, they are asking students to work to write up their ideas in a way that speaks compellingly to a real audience in a real publication forum. These teachers are creating communities of writers who take time with each other to shape ideas and craft them into effective prose. This is authentic writing. This is writing for the real.

AUTHENTIC TEACHING

Adherence to the inauthentic is the major barrier to relevance. With the best of intentions, we English teachers can find ourselves promoting topics that exist only in school and only for classrooms. We can find ourselves rewarding stilted, stale, and ineffective language. We can spend significant time teaching our students to include in their writing vocabulary words that function only on standardized tests. We can enforce archaic rules against ending sentences with prepositions and not splitting infinitives. We can ignore—and penalize in classroom work—the use of new words and phrases by dismissing them as slang and inappropriate. We can spend hours stamping out misused commas and apostrophes in an endless game of punctuation whack-a-mole. We can teach a kind of writing in utter disregard of the world clamoring outside our classroom. We can strangle the unique and creative voices developing in our classrooms right in front of us.

We could argue that today's current discourse mores are startling—indeed, with the changes in access to social media and the internet, not to mention the communication habits of our elected officials, much of what most of us have taught regarding acceptability, formality standards, and usage has been challenged, if not rendered quaintly obsolete. And, while we can and *should* certainly continue to maintain and teach standards of honesty and courtesy in our discourse, we would be lying if we continued to enforce with our students communication strictures from previous decades. The world spins merrily on, and most of that world is not paying attention to English class.

Instead, we must make English class relevant.

Thus we must bring the internet and social media into our classes; we must acknowledge and work with the changes in formality and acceptability. We must explore new words, new puns and double meanings, and acknowledge that gendered language is far more complex than the consistent use of *he* and *she;* cis gender and plural pronouns for singular individuals are not just the purview of the cognoscenti. We must accept and explore new terms for the variations we now see in race classifications and race designations. We must become aware of the many forms of English Language that function in the world, and infuse our teaching with a nuanced understanding of writing to different audiences for different purposes in different forums.

These are real—crucial, even—issues for our students and our world. Our authentic language and our authentic writing instruction demand that we respond.

Just as this book was going to press, we completed two professional development workshops based on the Continuing the Journey series. For four days, first in Rhode Island

and then in Louisiana, we explored with almost seventy veteran teachers the challenges and satisfactions of staying in the classroom. The participants in these workshops came from range of school settings, from rural Washington State to New York City, from Taiwan to Santo Domingo, from suburban communities in the Midwest and in the Deep South. What we found was that commonalities abound, and that for all these veteran teachers the commitment to their students and the strong sense of professionalism and expertise were considerable strengths. Asked to share their insights, the veteran teachers we worked with were fully aware of the challenges of today's education, but were also adept in their creative approaches and ways of making it new. It was, for us, an inspiring reaffirmation of the power of veteran teachers.

CONCLUSION: YOUTH EMPOWERED

Returning to a theme sounded in the beginning of this book, we once again acknowledge the new significance of the strong voices of young people. Speaking out against racism, homophobia, environmental neglect, anti-gun-legislation groups, and others, today's youth employ social media and, increasingly, mainstream television media to influence national debate. Our English classes and our schools can be an asset to these young people, whether they are finding their voices or refining their message. The evidence of these students is powerful and underscores the importance—and the moral inevitability—of teaching authentic language and writing in our classes and in our schools, in our classrooms and in our daily instruction.

Our students are on their own journeys as writers. We can try to steer them to a path that is straight and narrow by preparing them to approach writing as a simple set of rules and formulas. Or we can help them develop real-world, portable skills that will serve them well on any winding path they choose to take. As the world unfolds before them, they need to be prepared to meet it. As teachers, we are travelers along their journey, but they will pass us and move on to territories of their own. And if we have done a good job in our classrooms, their writing will be powerful, relevant, and authentic, and we as their teachers can be justifiably proud.

NOTES

1. Many of the ideas in this section are developed from our work in *Making the Journey: Being and Becoming a Teacher of English Language Arts*, 4th ed.

2. We are grateful to Belleview High School in Florida for granting us permission to reprint this rubric.

WORKS CITED

@AnneFrankCenter. "OUTRAGE! Teacher near Syracuse assigns defense of Holocaust; superintendent, NYS commissioner defend. FIRE THEM! #Antisemitism #neveragain." *Twitter*, 30 Mar. 2017, 1:42 p.m., https://www.twitter.com/AnneFrankCenter/status/847549508649177092.

@JenAnsbach. "I'm not sure why people are so surprised that the students are rising up – we've been feeding them a steady diet of dystopian literature showing teens leading the charge for years. We have told teen girls they are empowered. What, you thought it was fiction? It was preparation." *Twitter*, 18 Feb. 2018, 4:42 p.m., https://www.twitter.com/JenAnsbach/status/965385962925813761.

@Sarahchadwickk. "To every spokeswoman with an hourglass who uses free speech to alter and undermine what our flag represents...Your Time is running out. The clock starts now." -@sarahchad_ #MarchForOurLives." *Twitter*, 6 Mar. 2018, 3:06 p.m., https://www.twitter.com/Sarahchadwickk/status/971160230217297923.

@scott_zukowski. "This past semester, my students served as experiential learners at the @LIMuseum and turned their extensive archival research into 280 character posts for the museum's Twitter. Check it out! #teaching #sbu." *Twitter*, 2 Feb. 2018, 1:28 p.m., https://www.twitter.com/scott_zukowski/status/959538959494807552.

@wren_beth. "Hey @JenAnsbach Your sign went to VT's capital and met Katherine Paterson, children's laureate and author of Bridge to Terebithia. She loved it and I wanted you to know how many people were inspired by your words today. Thank you!! #marchforourlives." *Twitter*, 24 Mar. 2018, 3:38 p.m., https://www.twitter.com/wren_beth/status/977676163266072576.

Alda, Alan. *If I Understood You, Would I Have This Look on My Face? My Adventures in the Art and Science of Relating and Communicating.* New York: Random House, 2017. Print.

Andrade, Heidi G. "Understanding Rubrics." *Harvard.* 20 June 2014. PDF file. Web. https://www.saddleback.edu/uploads/goe/understanding_rubrics_by_heidi_goodrich_andrade.pdf.

Ansbach, Jennifer. *Take Charge of Your Teaching Evaluation: How to Grow Professionally and Get a Good Evaluation.* Portsmouth, NH: Heinemann, 2017. Print.

Bitzer, Lloyd F. "The Rhetorical Situation." *Philosophy & Rhetoric* 1.1 (1968): 1–14. Print.

Brannon, Lil, and C. H. Knoblauch. "On Students' Rights to Their Own Texts: A Model of Teacher Response." *College Composition and Communication* 33.2 (May 1982): 157–66. Print.

Bronfenbrenner, Urie. *The Ecology of Human Development: Experiments by Nature and Design.* Cambridge, MA: Harvard UP, 1979. Print.

———. *Making Human Beings Human: Bioecological Perspectives on Human Development.* Thousand Oaks, CA: Sage, 2005. Print.

Burke, Jim. "Connecting the Classroom, Community, and Curriculum." *English Journal* 101.4 (Mar. 2012): 17–28. Print.

———. *The English Teacher's Companion.* 4th ed. Portsmouth, NH: Heinemann, 2013. Print.

———. *What's the Big Idea? Question-Driven Units to Motivate Reading, Writing, and Thinking.* Portsmouth, NH: Heinemann, 2010. Print.

Christenbury, Leila. "Three Techniques of Student Evaluation." *How to Handle the Paper Load.* Ed. Gene Stanford. Urbana, IL: NCTE, 1979. 113–18. Print.

Christenbury, Leila, and Ken Lindblom. *Continuing the Journey: Becoming a Better Teacher of Literature and Informational Texts.* Urbana, IL: NCTE, 2017. Print.

———. *Making the Journey: Being and Becoming a Teacher of English Language Arts.* 4th ed. Portsmouth, NH: Heinemann, 2016. Print.

Clark, Romy, and Roz Ivanič. *The Politics of Writing.* London: Routledge, 1997. Print.

Cortez-Riggio, Kim-Marie. "The Green Footprint Project: How Middle School Students Inspired Their Community and Raised Their Self-Worth." *English Journal* 100.3 (Jan. 2011): 39–43. Print.

Council of Writing Program Administrators, National Council of Teachers of English, and National Writing Project. *Framework for Success in Postsecondary Writing.* Jan. 2011. PDF file. Web. http://wpacouncil.org/files/framework-for-success-postsecondary-writing.pdf.

Daiker, Donald A. "Learning to Praise." *Writing and Response: Theory, Practice, and Research.* Ed. Chris M. Anson. Urbana, IL: NCTE, 1989. 103–13. Print.

"Dana Loesch NRA Threat to Media: 'Your Time is Up'" *YouTube*, uploaded by Mitchell Wiggs. 6 Mar. 2018. Video file. Web. https://www.youtube.com/watch?v=LGxqdk4ylZs.

David, Ann D., Dorothy Meiburg Weller, and Amber Funderburgh. "Writing in the Work World." *Teachers, Profs, Parents: Writers Who Care.* 7 Oct. 2014. Web. https://writerswhocare.wordpress.com/2014/10/07/writing-in-the-work-world/.

Dean, Deborah. *Genre Theory: Teaching, Writing, and Being.* Urbana, IL: NCTE, 2008. Print.

———. *Strategic Writing: The Writing Process and Beyond in the Secondary English Classroom.* 2nd ed. Urbana, IL: NCTE, 2017. Print.

Dewar, Tim. "'I've Got Better Writing to Do.'" *Teachers, Profs, Parents: Writers Who Care.* 16 Mar. 2015. Web. https://writerswhocare.wordpress.com/2015/03/16/ive-got-better-writing-to-do/.

Dunn, Patricia A. "How to Promote Effective Peer Response." *Teaching and Learning in the SBU English Department.* Stony Brook University. 22 Mar. 2017. Blog. Web. https://you.stonybrook.edu/eglblog/2017/03/22/how-to-promote-effective-peer-response/#.WNPgZrSZQ4E.facebook.

———. *Talking, Sketching, Moving: Multiple Literacies in the Teaching of Writing.* Portsmouth, NH: Heinemann, 2001. Print.

Dunn, Patricia A., and Ken Lindblom. *Grammar Rants: How a Backstage Tour of Writing Complaints Can Help Students Make Informed, Savvy Choices about Their Writing.* Portsmouth, NH: Boynton/Cook, 2011. Print.

Ebert, Michael R. "Teen Creates Educational Water Safety Pamphlets." *Newsday.* 25 Mar. 2018, p. E19. Print.

Elbow, Peter. *Writing with Power: Techniques for Mastering the Writing Process.* 2nd ed. New York: Oxford UP, 1998. Print.

Emig, Janet A. "The Composing Process of Twelfth Graders." *NCTE Research Report No. 13.* Urbana, IL: NCTE, 1971. Print.

Esposito, Lauren. "Where to Begin? Using Place-Based Writing to Connect Students with Their Local Communities." *English Journal* 101.4 (Mar. 2012): 70–76. Print.

Fallows, James, and Deborah Fallows. *Our Towns: A 100,000-Mile Journey into the Heart of America.* New York: Pantheon, 2018. Print.

Freedman, Joel M. "Echoes of Silence: Empathy and Making Connections Through Writing Process." *English Journal* 98.4 (Mar. 2009): 92–95. Print.

Garner, Bryan A. *Garner's Modern American Usage: The Authority on Grammar, Usage, and Style.* 3rd ed. New York: Oxford UP, 2009. Print.

Gilyard, Keith. "Literacy, Identity, Imagination, Flight." *College Composition and Communication* 52.2 (Dec. 2000): 260–72. Print.

Goodwin, Bryan, and Kirsten Miller. "Research Says / Good Feedback Is Targeted, Specific, Timely." *Educational Leadership* 70.1 (Sep. 2012): 82–83. Print.

Hallman, Heidi L. "Authentic, Dialogic Writing: The Case of a Letter to the Editor." *English Journal* 98.5 (May 2009): 43–47. Print.

Hoover, M. R. "Community Attitudes toward Black English." *Language in Society* 7.1 (Apr. 1978): 65–87. Print.

Hopkins, Edwin M. "Can Good Composition Teaching Be Done under Present Conditions?" *English Journal* 1.1 (Jan. 1912): 1–8. Print.

Kahn, Elizabeth. "Making Writing Instruction Authentic." *English Journal* 98.5 (May 2009): 15–17. Print.

Kohn, Alfie. "Speaking My Mind: The Trouble with Rubrics." *English Journal* 95.4 (Mar. 2006): 12–15. Print.

Korb, Scott. "The Soul-Crushing Student Essay." *New York Times.* 21 Apr. 2018. Web. https://www.nytimes.com/2018/04/21/opinion/the-soul-crushing-student-essay.html.

Lenhart, Amanda, Sousan Arafeh, Aaron Smith, and Alexandra Macgill. "Writing, Technology and Teens." *Pew Research Center Report.* 24 Apr. 2008. Web. http://www.pewinternet.org/2008/04/24/writing-technology-and-teens/.

Levin, Nicole. "Teacher Asks Students to Debate in Favor of the Holocaust." *Attn.* 31 Mar. 2017. Web. https://www.attn.com/stories/16077/students-asked-debate-holocaust.

Lindblom, Ken. "Is Your Child Getting a Good Writing Education? Four Questions to Ask Your Child." *Teachers, Profs, Parents: Writers Who Care.* 30 May 2016. Web. https://writerswhocare.wordpress.com/2016/05/30/is-your-child-getting-a-good-writing-education-four-questions-to-ask-your-child/.

———. "Power Dynamics: Writing Up, Writing Down, Writing Across." *Teachers, Profs, Parents: Writers Who Care.* 13 Feb. 2017. Web. https://writerswhocare.wordpress.com/2017/02/13/power-dynamics-writing-up-writing-down-writing-across/.

———. "School Writing vs. Authentic Writing." *Teachers, Profs, Parents: Writers Who Care.* 27 Jul. 2015. Web. https://writerswhocare.wordpress.com/2015/07/27/school-writing-vs-authentic-writing/.

———. "Treating State Standardized Writing Tests as *Authentic* Writing Assignments." *English Leadership Quarterly* 30.2 (Oct. 2007): 10–11. Print.

———. "Writing for Real." *English Journal* 94.1 (Sept. 2004): 104–8. Print.

Lippi-Green, Rosina. *English with an Accent: Language, Ideology and Discrimination in the United States.* 2nd ed. New York: Routledge, 2012. Print.

Loretto, Adam, Sara DeMartino, and Amanda Godley. "Incorporating Students' Perspectives in the Design of Peer Review Activities." *Teachers, Profs, Parents: Writers Who Care.* 2 Apr. 2018. Web. https://writerswhocare.wordpress.com/2018/04/02/incorporating-students-perspectives-in-the-design-of-peer-review-activities/.

Lu, Min-Zahn, and Bruce Horner. "The Logic of Listening to Global Englishes." *Code-Meshing as World English: Pedagogy, Policy, Performance.* Eds. Vershawn Ashanti Young and Aja Y. Martinez. Urbana, IL: NCTE, 2011. Print.

Mack, Nancy. "Colorful Revision: Color-Coded Comments Connected to Instruction." *Teaching English in the Two-Year College* 40.3 (Mar. 2013): 248–56. Print.

———. *Engaging Writers with Multigenre Research Projects: A Teacher's Guide.* New York: Teachers College Press, 2015. Print.

Macrorie, Ken. *Telling Writing.* Rochelle Park, NJ: Hayden, 1970. Print.

Marchetti, Allison, and Rebekah O'Dell. *Beyond Literary Analysis: Teaching Students to Write with Passion and Authority about Any Text.* Portsmouth, NH: Heinemann, 2018. Print.

McMahon, Julie. "NY Education Chief Sees How Nazi Essay Could Prompt Critical Thinking." *Syracuse.com.* 30 Mar. 2017, updated 31 Mar. 2017. Web. http://www.syracuse.com/schools/index.ssf/2017/03/nazi_holocaust_homework_assignment_new_york_education_commissioner_maryellen_eli.html.

Menand, Louis. "Words of the Year." *The New Yorker.* 8 Jan. 2018. Web. https://www.newyorker.com/magazine/2018/01/08/words-of-the-year.

Nakashima, Ryan. "Liked Raw Carrots, Hated Green Beans." *The Seattle Times.* 31 July 2007. Web. https://www.seattletimes.com/nation-world/liked-raw-carrots-hated-green-beans/.

National Council of Teachers of English. *NCTE/IRA Standards for the English Language Arts.* 2012. Web. http://www.ncte.org/standards/ncte-ira.

——. *Professional Knowledge for the Teaching of Writing.* 28 Feb. 2016. Web. http://www2.ncte.org/statement/teaching-writing/.

——. "Rhetorical Situation." *College Composition and Communication.* 2010. Web. http://www.ncte.org/library/NCTEFiles/Resources/Journals/CCC/0613-feb2010/CCC0613Poster.pdf.

Newkirk, Thomas. *Embarrassment: And the Emotional Underlife of Learning.* Portsmouth, NH: Heinemann, 2017. Print.

Neyer, Janet. "Know the Power of Your Audience!" 2017. PDF file. Web. https://drive.google.com/file/d/0B13or2y50_90ZThwaTZodW4tdTA/view.

Nixon, Amy Ash. *Caledonian-Record.* "School Project Encourages Community Engagement in Vermont." *U.S. News & World Report.* 19 Mar. 2018. Web. https://www.usnews.com/news/best-states/vermont/articles/2018-03-19/school-project-encourages-community-engagement-in-vermont?int=undefined-rec.

——. "Students Create 'Humans of Burke' Exhibit." *Caledonian Record.* 19 Mar. 2018. Web. http://www.caledonianrecord.com/news/local/humans-of-burke-exhibit-opens-at-cafe-lotti-wednesday/article_8e101edd-16b5-5ed5-9c41-c243949826b4.html.

Rademacher, Tom. *It Won't Be Easy: An Exceedingly Honest (and Slightly Unprofessional) Love Letter to Teaching.* Minneapolis, MN: University of Minnesota Press, 2017. Print.

——. "My Name Is Tom. I've Been a Teacher for 10 Years and I Still Get My Ass Kicked Nearly Every Day." *educationpost.* 20 Apr. 2017. Blog. Web. http://educationpost.org/my-name-is-tom-ive-been-a-teacher-for-10-years-and-i-still-get-my-ass-kicked-nearly-every-day/.

Roseboro, Anna J. Small. "Writing—In-Class Peer Feedback." *Teaching English Language Arts.* 16 Mar. 2017. Blog. Web. http://teachingenglishlanguagearts.com/writing-in-class-peer-feedback/.

Schuster, Edgar H. *Breaking the Rules: Liberating Writers Through Innovative Grammar Instruction.* Portsmouth, NH: Heinemann, 2003. Print.

Shaughnessy, Mina P. *Errors and Expectations: A Guide for the Teacher of Basic Writing.* New York: Oxford UP, 1977. Print.

Sieben, Nicole. *Writing Hope Strategies for Writing Success in Secondary Schools: A Strengths-Based Approach to Teaching Writing.* Boston, MA: Brill Sense, 2018. Print.

Siegal, Allan M., and William G. Connolly. *The New York Times Manual of Style and Usage: The Official Style Guide Used by the Writers and Editors of the World's Most Authoritative News Organization.* 5th ed. New York: Three Rivers Press, 2015. Print.

Slusher, Brian. "Praising, Questioning, Wishing: An Approach to Responding to Writing." *NWP National Writing Project.* 4 May 2009. Web. https://www.nwp.org/cs/public/print/resource/2868.

Smitherman, Geneva. "'The Blacker the Berry, the Sweeter the Juice': African American Student Writers and the National Assessment of Educational Progress." National Council of Teachers of English Annual Convention. Pittsburgh, PA, November 1993. Print.

——. *Talkin and Testifyin: The Language of Black America.* Detroit, MI: Wayne State UP, 1986. Print.

Sommers, Nancy. "Responding to Student Writing." *College Composition and Communication* 33.2 (May 1982): 148–6. Print.

Stanford, Gene, and the [NCTE] Committee on Classroom Practices. *How to Handle the Paper Load.* Urbana, IL: NCTE, 1979. Print.

Steineke, Nancy. *Assessment Live! 10 Real-Time Ways for Kids to Show What They Know—and Meet the Standards.* Portsmouth, NH: Heinemann, 2009. Print.

Sun Sentinel. "Stoneman Douglas Student Sarah Chadwick Turns the Tables on That Ominous NRA Ad." *YouTube.* 9 Mar. 2018. Video file. Web. https://www.youtube.com/watch?v=yr-hkk3CWvU.

Thomas, P. L. "De-grading Writing Instruction: Closing the 'Considerable Gap.'" *De-testing and De-grading Schools: Authentic Alternatives to Accountability and Standardization.* Eds. Joe Bower and P. L. Thomas. New York: Peter Lang, 2016. Print.

Wheeler, Rebecca S. "Code-Switch to Teach Standard English." *English Journal* 94.5 (May 2005): 108–12. Print.

Wiggins, Grant. "Real-World Writing: Making Purpose and Audience Matter." *English Journal* 98.5 (May 2009): 29–37. Print.

———. "Seven Keys to Effective Feedback." *Educational Leadership* 70.1 (Sep. 2012): 10–16. Print.

Wilson, Maja. "Why I Won't Be Using Rubrics to Respond to Students' Writing." *English Journal* 96.4 (Mar. 2007): 62–66. Print.

Winn, Maisha T., and Latrise P. Johnson. *Writing Instruction in the Culturally Relevant Classroom.* Urbana, IL: NCTE, 2011. Print.

Wong, Alia. "The Parkland Students Aren't Going Away." *The Atlantic.* 24 Feb. 2018. Web. https://www.theatlantic.com/education/archive/2018/02/the-parkland-students-arent-going-away/554159/.

Yancey, Kathleen Blake. *Portfolios in the Writing Classroom: An Introduction.* Urbana, IL: NCTE, 1992. Print.

Young, Vershawn Ashanti. "Should Writers Use They Own English?" *Iowa Journal of Cultural Studies* 12.1 (2010): 110–17. Print.

Young, Vershawn Ashanti, Rusty Barrett, Y'Shanda Young-Rivera, and Kim Brian Lovejoy. *Other People's English: Code-Meshing, Code-Switching, and African American Literacy.* New York: Teachers College P, 2014. Print.

INDEX

AUTHORS

KEN LINDBLOM is associate professor of English and, until recently, served as dean of the School of Professional Development at Stony Brook University and led the university's teacher and leader education programs. He currently teaches courses in English, rhetoric, and communication. A member of NCTE since 1989, Ken was editor of *English Journal* from 2008 to 2013. He is coauthor of three other books about teaching English and has published more than two dozen articles, book chapters, and peer reviewed blog posts on the subject. His tenth-grade sense of humor wins him equal numbers of friends and enemies, which is better odds than he deserves. He can be contacted at kenneth.lindblom@stonybrook.edu and @klind2013, and he blogs at https://edukention.wordpress.com/.

LEILA CHRISTENBURY is Emerita Commonwealth Professor of English Education at Virginia Commonwealth University, Richmond, where she has taught English methods, young adult literature, applied English linguistics, and the teaching of writing. For seven years she was director of the Capital Writing Project, a site of the National Writing Project. A past president of the NCTE and a past editor of *English Journal*, her research has been recognized by the David H. Russell Award for Distinguished Research in the Teaching of English; the James N. Britton Award for Inquiry in English Language Arts; and the Edward B. Fry Book Award for Outstanding Contributions to Literacy Research. An active member of NCTE for more than 40 years, she taught in Virginia schools and universities for most of her career. She is the author, coauthor, or editor of 14 books and the author of approximately 100 chapters and articles on the teaching of English. She can be contacted at lchriste@vcu.edu and leilachristenbury@gmail.com.

JENNIFER ANSBACH, a National Board Certified Teacher, teaches English at Manchester Township High School in New Jersey and is pursuing a PhD in American studies at Rutgers University. You can often find her on the sofa curled up with tea and a book. Her new book is *Take Charge of Your Teaching Evaluation: How to Grow Professionally and Get a Good Evaluation* (2018). When she's not reading, she's tweeting at @JenAnsbach.

JIM BURKE teaches at Burlingame High School in California and is the author of numerous bestselling books about teaching English, including *The English Teacher's Companion* (4th ed.) and *What's the Big Idea?* He is the founder of the English Companion Ning and the resource-rich website www.english companion.com. Burke has received numerous awards, including the NCTE Intellectual Freedom Award, the NCTE Conference on English Leadership Award, and the California Reading Association Hall of Fame Award. Join his more than 25,000 followers at @englishcomp.

DEBORAH DEAN is a former secondary teacher who now teaches preservice teachers at Brigham Young University. She is the author of many articles in NCTE journals and several books about writing, including *Strategic Writing* (2nd ed.); *Genre Theory: Teaching, Writing, and Being; What Works in Writing Instruction;* and *Revision Decisions* (with Jeff Anderson).

PATRICIA A. DUNN is professor of English at Stony Brook University in New York, where she teaches courses in writing theory and practice. She has published a number of books, articles, and blogs on the teaching of writing, among them *Talking, Sketching, Moving: Multiple Literacies in the Teaching of Writing* (2001). Her first book, *Learning Re-Abled: The Learning Disability Controversy and Composition Studies* (1995), is now available online for free at the WAC Clearinghouse. She can be reached at patricia.dunn@stonybrook.edu or @PatriciaDunn1.

ELLEN FOLEY is a former high school English instructor, literacy coach, reading specialist, and National Board Certified Teacher. She is currently pursuing her PhD in English education at Western Michigan University. Email her at ellen.foley@wmich.edu or contact her on Twitter at @ellenjanefoley.

LORENA GERMÁN is a thirteenth-year Dominican American educator working with young people in Austin, Texas. She has been published by NCTE, ASCD, *EdWeek*, and others. Her undergraduate degree is from Emmanuel College, her graduate degree is from the Bread Loaf School of English at Middlebury, Vermont, and she is a member of the Bread Loaf Teacher Network. She was the recipient of NCTE's Early Career Educator of Color Leadership Award and winner of NCTE's Latinx Caucus Excelencia in Teaching Scholarship Award. Germán is the incoming Chair of NCTE's Committee Against Racism and Bias in the Teaching of English. She also co-founded The Multicultural Classroom, an organization seeking to support educators in developing a culturally sustaining approach to education. She is a wife, mami, and writer. Contact her on Twitter at @nenagerman.

NANCY MACK is a professor emeritus of English at Wright State University and the author of *Engaging Writers with Multigenre Research Projects* (2015) and two volumes about teaching grammar with poetry. She edited a special issue of *English Journal* (July 2012) about bullying and has published several articles and chapters on memoir, emotional labor, the working class, and composition theories.

ALISON MCKEOUGH graduated from Stony Brook University and has been teaching at Patchogue-Medford High School on Long Island, New York, for nine years. She has taught secondary ELA and been the co-advisor of the high school newspaper, *The Red & Black*, and its broadcast station, Raider TV. McKeough currently teaches AP Language, English 11, Suspense & the Supernatural, and Heroes & Villains: Adventures in Fantasy.

KIMBERLY N. PARKER, who earned a PhD from the University of Illinois at Urbana–Champaign, currently works with preservice teachers as assistant director of teacher training at the Shady Hill School in Cambridge, Massachusetts. Parker taught English in public schools for 17 years and served on several committees for NCTE. She was a Heinemann Fellow, and her ongoing work explores the literacy lives of Black youth. Contact her at @TchKimpossible and email her at kimpossible97@gmail.com.

EVELYN T. PINEIRO started her career at Random House Publishing Group and then taught high school literature classes at Sacred Heart Academy in Hempstead, New York. She eventually made her home at Oceanside Middle School on Long Island, New York, where she has taught English for the past ten years. Pineiro has presented at various regional and national conferences on using technology to make classrooms more student centered. She can be reached at writewithvoice@gmail.com.

DAWN REED is an English teacher at Okemos High School in Okemos, Michigan, and a co-director of the Red Cedar Writing Project at Michigan State University, a site of the National Writing Project. She also conducts professional development for teachers focused on technology integration and the teaching of writing. Reed is coauthor of *Research Writing Rewired: Lessons That Ground Students' Digital Learning* (2015) and *Real Writing: Modernizing the Old School Essay* (2016) and has published in various journals, books, and websites. Follow Dawn on Twitter at @dawnreed.

CHRISTOPHER SCANLON has been identified by the Florida Department of Education as one of the highest impact teachers in the state, and he has received the "Best and Brightest" Teacher Scholarship award from FLDOE three years in a row. Just the same, he feels like he still has a lot to learn. In his largely theoretical spare time, he enjoys reading and photography. Reach him at @ScanlonFL or christopher.scanlon@marion.k12.fl.us.

ANDY SCHOENBORN is a high school English teacher in Michigan at Mt. Pleasant public schools. He focuses his work on progressive literacy methods, including student-centered critical thinking, digital collaboration, and professional development. As a past president of the Michigan Council of Teachers of English and a National Writing Project teacher consultant for Central Michigan University's Chippewa River Writing Project, he frequently conducts workshops related to literacy and technology. Read his thoughts on literacy in the elafieldbook.wordpress.com and follow him on Twitter at @aschoenborn.

NICOLE SIEBEN is assistant professor of secondary English education at the State University of New York College at Old Westbury, where she is also the coordinator for the graduate programs in English education. A former high school English teacher in New York public schools, Sieben's research focuses on building "writing hope" in secondary and postsecondary education, social justice practices, and professional development in K–12 schools. Her book, *Writing Hope Strategies for Writing Success in Secondary Schools* (2018), elaborates on the aforementioned theory of writing hope and its classroom applications. She can be reached at Siebenn@oldwestbury.edu and @Teach4JusticeNS.

JULIA TORRES has taught language arts for 13 years and currently teaches AP English Language and Composition and AP English Literature and Composition at a public high school in Denver, Colorado. As a teacher-activist committed to education as a practice of freedom, her teaching is grounded in the work of empowering students to use language arts to fuel resistance and positive social transformation. Torres facilitates workshops and professional conversations about antibias/antiracist education, social justice, and culturally sustaining pedagogies; she also serves on several local and national boards and committees promoting educational equity and progressivism. Contact her at @juliaerin80.

Y'SHANDA YOUNG-RIVERA is a state-certified teacher and administrator and a current PhD candidate at Northwestern University's School of Education and Social Policy. She has more than 20 years of experience teaching, training, designing curriculum, and implementing professional development in urban education settings. Her research involves improving educational and social outcomes for low socioeconomic status minority students via cultural ecological frameworks that include design of learning environments, critical literacy engagement, and identity development. She coauthored *Other People's English: Code-Meshing, Code-Switching and African American Literacy* (2014). Young-Rivera can be reached at yshandarivera@u.northwestern.edu.

This book was typeset in Calluna and Saira by Barbara Frazier.

Typefaces used on the cover include Joe Hand 2, Galaxie Polaris, and Gill Sans MT.

The book was printed on 50-lb. White Offset paper by Versa Press, Inc.